CH00706764

The Lincolnshire Potato Railways

by
Stewart E. Squires

THE OAKWOOD PRESS

First Edition published 1987
Second Revised Edition 2005

British Library Cataloguing in Publication Data
A Record for this book is available from the British Library
ISBN 0 85361 646 9

Typeset by Oakwood Graphics.
Repro by PKmediaworks, Cranborne, Dorset.
Printed by Cambrian Printers, Aberystwyth, Ceredigion.

The Great Northern Railway sidings in Boston used for the concentration and dispatch of the south Lincolnshire potato traffic, in 1916.   *Railway Magazine*

Published by The Oakwood Press (Usk), P.O. Box 13, Usk, Mon., NP15 1YS.
E-mail: sales@oakwoodpress.co.uk
Website: www.oakwoodpress.co.uk

Contents

	Introduction	4
Chapter One	The Fens and Marsh of Lincolnshire	5
Chapter Two	Railways and Farming	9
Chapter Three	Railways for Reclamation and Drainage	15
Chapter Four	Potato Railways: Rise and Decline	21
Chapter Five	The Farm Railways Described	27
Chapter Six	The Dennis Locomotives	131
Chapter Seven	The Nocton Rolling Stock	135
Chapter Eight	Potato Railways - The Successors	139
Appendix One	List of Lincolnshire Potato Railways	152
Appendix Two	The Bishopthorpe Wagon and Francis Theakston	155
Appendix Three	Christian & Dobbs	157
	Acknowledgements to First Edition	159
	Acknowledgements to New Edition	160

List of Tables

Table One	Lister Diesels used at North Sea Camp	17
Table Two	River Board Locomotives	20
Table Three	Sugar Beet Delivered to the Bardney Factory by the Nocton Estate Railway, 1927 to 1951	53
Table Four	Nocton Rolling Stock and Valuation, 1947	75
Table Five	Nocton Rolling Stock and Valuation, 1964	77
Table Six	Locomotive Fleet, Nocton Light Railway	134

Introduction

Lincolnshire and South Humberside is an area not noted for its narrow gauge railways. From the time of the Industrial Revolution through to modern times it has had many short lengths of line serving brickworks, sand and gravel quarries, ironstone mines, and limestone quarries, just as has been the case countrywide. In addition, in Lincolnshire, they were also found in bulbfields and nurseries in the Spalding Area and serving the RAF bombing and gunnery ranges at Sutton Bridge.

What is much less known is the extent of the use such lines were put to on farms, but this is where the area made its greatest use of them. It is not generally appreciated that over 140 route miles of track were laid on farms in at least 50 separate locations, from Alkborough on the banks of the River Humber to Crowland in the south.

They were a phenomenon of the Fenland, and, it must be said, not confined to Lincolnshire. However, their use in other counties may not have been as widespread. In agricultural terms, they were also used to serve bulb fields in the Spalding area, but this book is confined to their use mainly for the planting and the harvest of probably one of the County's best known products of the 20th century, the humble potato.

It is because the railways are so little known, and because time will naturally take its toll of those who knew and worked on them, that it is appropriate that this book should be devoted to them.

It is interesting to surmise why they are so little known, especially in view of the present day nostalgia for railways. Old maps often refer to them as tramways, so it may be that they are not considered to be true railways. But if a railway is a transport system on which trains run on rails then they meet the definition. Anyway, there is also a great nostalgia for tramways, albeit mainly the urban street variety. Perhaps it is because they carried no passengers, had no signals and were built almost entirely on private land, although several crossed the public highway on the level. Many were of very short length, and used horses as their motive power. Others were longer, long enough in fact to employ the use of internal combustion engines, and even small steam engines. It is noticeable that the only ones on which articles have appeared in specialist journals have been some of the latter, with notes on the motive power used. These, too, are the only ones of which contemporary photographic evidence tends to remain and this gives the best clue. It seems that the use of some sort of locomotive on a substantial length of track is the criteria for sparking off the limited interest there has been in them in the past.

Knowledge of the date of construction of many of the lines is limited but they did give sterling service to the farmers who used them for around 60 years from the turn of the 20th century, and their history deserves to be written.

In common with narrow gauge lines in many other parts of England, none now survive. However, all was not lost as track, engines and rolling stock from one of them, at Nocton, survived to create a new line, the Lincolnshire Coast Light Railway near Cleethorpes, albeit in a new guise, that of a passenger-carrying narrow gauge railway. This has since closed but the railway lives on and is being revived at Winthorpe, near Skegness.

This history includes railways on 50 farms. Finding this number has not been an easy task, as many came and went without being recorded on contemporary maps. The existence of others cannot be entirely ruled out.

Chapter One

The Fens and Marsh of Lincolnshire

The Fenlands of Lincolnshire comprise about one-third of the area of the County, the second largest in England. They comprise all of the south-east section of the County, with a long tongue reaching north and west, following the valley of the River Witham, to reach the edge of the County town, Lincoln. Right up in the north-west corner of Lincolnshire is the Isle of Axholme, another area of largely low lying landscape at the confluence of the Rivers Trent and Ouse, where they combine to form the River Humber.

Until their drainage began in the 1600s they were low lying, marshy areas, poorly drained, whose inhabitants suffered from various fevers while engaged in cattle rearing and wildfowling. Large areas close to the Wash suffered periodic inundations of the sea.

Over the course of three centuries they were successively drained. Rivers were diverted, new drains cut, sea banks built to claim new land, enabling their use initially for pasture, but increasingly for arable crops. Today grain, potatoes, sugar beet, vegetables, salad crops, bulbs and soft fruit are grown almost exclusively, the dark loamy soil being among the most fertile in the land.

Drainage of the Fens was not accomplished overnight. An unfortunate side effect of the improvements, particularly on peat fens, was that as the soils dried out they shrank, and in some cases the land, always barely above sea level, fell below it. Pumps were required to lift water from one level to another. At first this was done with windmills, later, from the 1850s, by steam engines, and is now done by electricity. However, over the centuries it was a constant struggle to keep the land above water, and there were reverses as pumps failed and river banks were breached.

Generally, the Fens on which farm railways were built were those most recently reclaimed. South Moor at West Butterwick was reclaimed between 1837 and 1846. Deeping St Nicholas was created in 1846 out of Deeping Fen marking the culmination of almost 300 years of effort. In the 1860s the new land between Holbeach and The Wash was populated, celebrated by the building of churches at Holbeach Hurn in 1871, and Holbeach St Marks and Holbeach St Matthew in 1869.

What is known in Lincolnshire as the Marsh is the strip of land between the Lincolnshire Wolds and the North Sea, from Skegness in the south to the River Humber, beyond Grimsby, in the north. It is around 50 miles in length, varying in width from two to five miles. It is land that has always been protected from the sea, as it is today, by a line of sandhills lining the back of the sandy beaches. Parts of it are, however, below sea level due to successive reclamations from the 17th to the 20th centuries. This can be appreciated most dramatically from the top of the dunes, north of Donna Nook. 20,000 acres of land were flooded in the storm surge of 1953 since which time much energy has been expended in maintaining and improving flood defences to avoid a repeat.

The fresh water marshes have now long disappeared, but the saltmarsh around the edge of the Wash continued to be reclaimed and new farmland brought into production up to 1980. Proposals for a Wash barrage with large scale reclamation, as has happened in Holland, are talked about from time to time, but the value of this area for wildlife is likely to protect it from this for the foreseeable future. Indeed, the 21st century has seen the beginning of a new process known as Managed Retreat. This involves the breaching of some banks to allow the sea to reclaim the foreshore for the benefit of the wildlife.

Farming in the Fens and Marsh

At the dawn of the 20th century land which up to 40 years before had been a marsh was being successfully farmed. It had not only been a case of draining this land to make it agriculturally viable, for hand-in-hand with draining had to go the building of homesteads for the farmers, small hamlets or groups of cottages for the labourers, and new roads to serve them. Examples of these newer communities referred to in this book are Holbeach St Marks, Holbeach St Matthew and Dawsmere, the two latter places founded on land reclaimed in the late 18th century and the former in the 17th century.

Farming at this time was labour intensive for the mixed system followed involved the tending, breeding and fattening of livestock, as well as cultivating the soil. The prime mover was the horse though there was some steam cultivation. Men had to live near the animals to look after them properly, so that, as well as the sizeable villages, there was also a considerable scattered population.

Hard surfaced roads, passable in all weathers, were needed to serve them and to link the farmsteads with the marketing points for the produce so that it could be sold. Away from these hard roads on the actual farms, cart tracks linked the buildings with the flat, open fields. Relying as they did largely on man-made drainage, usually involving pumping, it should come as no surprise to realise that during the winter months the fields were often a quagmire in which conventional haulage methods encountered great difficulties. An illustration of

Caudwells Farm, Grainthorpe. Pea vining taking place at 'Tin Town'. The pea vines are being forked off narrow gauge wagons. At the lower right the chain coupling can be seen. *Ian Rowson*

the problem comes from the previous century. In 1865, Walter White, on a tour of the Fens, noted in the Sutton Bridge area:

In a country where thousands of acres are below the level of the sea, and the maintenance of land depends on a ceaseless contest with water, one would hardly look for the ordinary breed. The banks which cross all the landscapes with dark lines, straight or curved, are the only roads, now for the most part hard roads; but twenty or even ten years ago these were sludgy tracks. Some remember the time when the ruts were 'just the same as ditches, deeper than wagon wheels and the wheels did not turn round, they only slid along on the hub'. A small proprietor could not afford to spend money in road making, and so got out of the difficulty by harnessing eight or ten horses to a laden wagon which two could draw when they came to a hard road. And in wet weather, or during a thaw, no one could ride or walk along the banks without a thick bespattering from head to foot.

It was to solve this transport problem that the landowners turned to the use of light railways. Having built them to serve the needs of the potato industry, they would also be used for the other crops produced on the farm.

The shape of many of the farms suited the application of railways. The boundaries being set in more modern times on land divided into rectangular blocks by drainage dykes meant that generally the farms were long and rectangular. Indeed, on Deeping Fen, they tended to be of two fields width, their length being the distance between drains. A railway down the centre served the whole farm. On larger farms the rails spread out from the farmstead like the spokes of a wheel. The presence of dykes did not constitute any great problem either, as fields on the opposite bank to a dykeside line could be served by a temporary plank bridge at a convenient point.

Of the fertility of the land there can be no doubt. In the 1920s south-east Lincolnshire dispatched two to four hundred railway wagonloads of potatoes each day for six months of the year to destinations countrywide. The potato season started each year with new potatoes in July and August, and the main crop followed from September to April. They are a heavy bulk crop and growers had problems getting them to market. The fields in which they were grown were spread throughout the district, often far from the nearest railway station. The railway companies encouraged the development of the trade by making generous allowances to cover the cost of cartage to the stations, and organised the onward transhipment from there, often at special rates. From the wayside stations loaded wagons were taken to Boston and Spalding which became the major dispatch centres. Here, the wagons were sorted for distribution countrywide, and to the docks for export. In 1916 the principal destination was London, for the metropolis, and the South and West of England. Others were Newcastle, Leeds, Sheffield, Manchester and Liverpool. Exports were sent to the docks at London, Hull, Southampton and Liverpool. At the beginning of the season the traffic was so heavy that the six or seven daily trains had to be doubled or even trebled, and a vegetable 'train' from Boston to London could consist of up to six trains.

In the 1930s one Fleet farm dispatched 17,000 tons of produce annually. This figure was made up of 10,000 tons of potatoes, 1,500 tons of grain, 4,500 tons of sugar beet, and 1,000 tons of other produce. In addition, 2,000 tons of fertiliser, seed potatoes and cereal seeds were received, and in the mid-1950s, the Nocton Estate produced 17,000 tons of food, mainly potatoes, each year.

Potatoes, both loose and in sacks, being loaded at a Lincolnshire station early in 1916.
Railway Magazine

Potatoes delivered to the goods yard in sacks by horse and cart are emptied into wagons.
This photograph dates from 1916 and was probably taken at Boston.   *Railway Magazine*

Chapter Two

Railways and Farming

The history of the use of rails on farms is a long one, almost as old as the history of railways themselves. An early record appeared in *The Times* in 1850, when Sir James Caird reported:

> The farm of Mr Neilson, of Halewood, exhibits several points worthy of notice. A light tramway with wagons is made use of for taking the turnip crop off the ground in moist weather. The tramway is readily shifted, and the crop is thrown into the wagons, which are then each pushed along by a man, so that the entire crop may be removed from the ground, which receives no injury from the feet of the horses. The tramway can be constructed for 1s. 4d. per yard, and might be very advantageously introduced on all heavy farms where it is found difficult to take off the turnip crop in moist weather. A gang of men are at present employed on a considerable field of Mr Neilson's in taking off the turnip crop, which they draw from the ground, fill into the wagons, and convey outside the gate at a rate of 6s. an acre, shifting the tramway at their own cost. At this work they earn 2s. 3d. a day.

The Halewood referred to is probably the village near Liverpool. It was not Lincolnshire. In the 1850s the growing of turnips was a much greater industry than that of potatoes but the problem of getting onto and off the land in wet conditions was just the same.

In 1863 J.B. Denton, writing in *Farm Homesteads of England,* described how the buildings on a Hertfordshire farm of 614 acres included a tramway serving a fixed steam threshing machine. Wagons brought in the stacks and took out the grain and straw. This was a variation on the earlier use in that the rails did not go into the fields. It was not uncommon for a Victorian High Farm of the steam age to have a tramway around the buildings. There were two examples, at least, of these in Lincolnshire. One was at Moses Farm at Stenigot and another at Stourton Home Farm near Baumber.

Throughout the last half of the 19th century the network of Victorian railways spread quickly around Britain. They were not promoted solely to benefit agriculture although the Prospectus of almost every line argued for the benefits that would accrue to the agriculture of the district through which they ran. Farms were rarely served directly. Instead, farmers made use of the many wayside village stations. This meant that they had to cart their fertilizers and crops to and from their fields.

Towards the end of the 19th century it was becoming clear to the Government that there were many areas of the country which, because they were not served by a nearby line, did not benefit from railways. At this time it was said that no town or village in England was more than 10 miles from a railway station. In Lincolnshire only a small handful of settlements were over five miles away. These areas were almost all rural districts which had only agriculture as a local industry. The Light Railways Act of 1896 was the result. Lightly laid lines, having speed and weight restrictions with minimal signalling and minimal station platforms, were promoted.

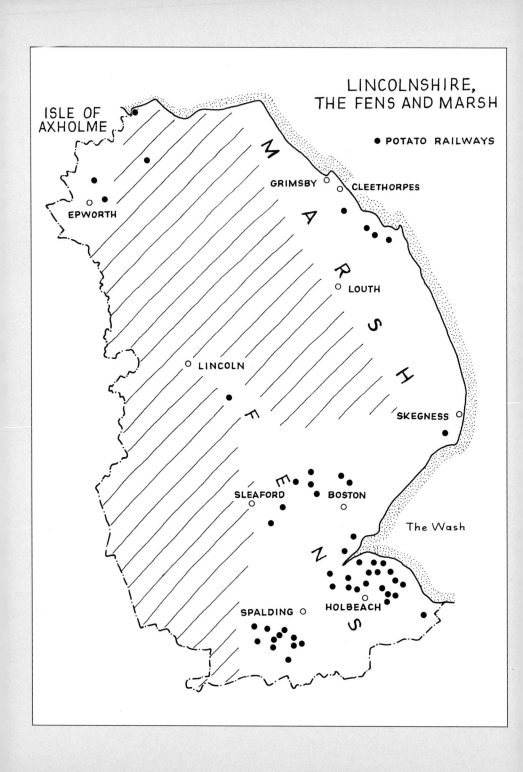

ISLE OF
AXHOLME

LINCOLNSHIRE,
THE FENS AND MARSH

● POTATO RAILWAYS

EPWORTH

GRIMSBY   CLEETHORPES

M
A
R
S
H

LOUTH

LINCOLN

F
E
N

SKEGNESS

SLEAFORD   BOSTON

The Wash

SPALDING   HOLBEACH

S

The railways built as a result of this legislation, certainly in the beginning, were of standard gauge. This was logical in that problems of later transhipment between gauges was avoided. The Leek & Manifold Valley Light Railway of 1904 adopted one solution. This narrow gauge line used transporter wagons, narrow gauge trucks with a flat bed on which ran standard gauge rails. These then carried standard gauge vehicles, rolled on and off at the junction of the two gauges, at Leek.

The Benwick Goods branch, 1898, and the Axholme Joint Railway, 1900-1909, were examples of standard gauge lines built at this time with the improvement of agriculture as an aim. The Axholme Joint Railway provided, in addition to its nine conventional stations, no less than 20 goods depots and sidings. Of these 16 served individual or groups of farms.

These were conventional railways in that they provided a standard gauge railway facility in the traditional manner, to those farms alongside or near to their sidings and depots. The only major light railway built to penetrate to the individual farms themselves, and built only to serve those farms, was the Wissington Light Railway of 1905. This, 20 miles in extent, was built on private land on the Wissington and Methwold Fens and, therefore, was exempt from the need for any Act of Parliament.

A number of light railway schemes were promoted for the benefit of agriculture in the Fens east of Spalding. The Great Northern Railway (GNR) and the Midland & Great Northern Joint Railway (M&GN), served the area, and a number of routes to act as direct feeders to their existing stations were proposed but none were built.

The earliest of these was the Spalding & South Lincolnshire Light Railway, promoted in 1897 by a group of Spalding businessmen. It was to be a 2 ft 6 in. narrow gauge line, running in a 25 mile loop from the M&GN immediately east of Spalding, northwards to Moulton Seas End, across Whaplode, Holbeach and Gedney Marshes, to the River Nene almost at its mouth, and then south along the riverbank to a terminus adjacent to Sutton Bridge Dock. Steam-hauled trains would provide both passenger and goods services, and farms would be served with their own sidings. At the River Nene it would connect with its own landing stage for goods transfer to boats.

Many more schemes were promoted immediately after World War I. In 1919 W. Alban Richards and Co., Engineers and Contractors, produced a plan of the proposed Holland Light Railways. (They were in the area of Holland County Council, so named because it resembled the landscape of that country.) This proposed a number of standard gauge light railways; Boston to Wrangle via Frieston; Donington station on the Great Northern & Great Eastern Joint Railway (GN&GEJR) to Counter Drain on the M&GN, along the South Forty Foot Drain; North Drove, M&GN, to Deeping Fen; a loop from Littleworth to Deeping St James GNR stations, via Crowland Common and the River Welland, with a branch northwards alongside the South Drove Drain; Eye, M&GN, to Crowland; Moulton station, M&GN, to Whaplode Marsh, with a branch from Moulton Seas End on to Weston Marsh; Holbeach, M&GN, north to Holbeach St Marks, and south to Sutton St James; Gedney, M&GN, to Gedney Marsh with a branch to Lutton Marsh; and French Drove, GN&GEJR, to Tydd St Giles, with a branch from Gedney Hill to Holbeach Drove. Together with existing railways this network would have meant that very few Fenland farms would have been more than two miles away from a railway.

By 1920 these proposals had evolved with the resurrection of a loop around the north of Holbeach similar to that of 1897, but now standard gauge and running from Weston station on the M&GN, to Sutton Bridge, replacing the three branches running north from M&GN stations. The Boston line would have extended to Wainfleet, and the proposals for routes to Sutton St James, Gedney Hill and Holbeach Drove were replaced with one from Cowbit, GN&GEJR, to Wisbech St Mary, M&GN. Three routes were replaced with proposed narrow gauge lines: Twenty, M&GN, to Quadring on the GN&GEJR, replacing Donington to Counter Drain; North Drove, along North Drove Drain for a greater distance; and south from Littleworth to South Drove Drain, the Deeping St James extension being dropped.

None of these were proceeded with. By this time there was an increasing use of road transport, many lorries being bought from Army surplus depots by farmers. A rural transport revolution was underway and these early beginnings would, in time, cause the closure of much of the existing Fenland railway mileage. Even if they had been built they would have not replaced the need for the farm narrow gauge railways. Some of the latter may not have been so extensive, but they would have run to the nearest railway siding, instead of the nearest road. Perhaps the only line to be built which mirrored these proposals was the Fleet Light Railway and its extensions, a narrow gauge line running northwards from Fleet station (*see Chapter Five, 34: Fleet Light Railway*).

Narrow gauge railways serving farms were very rare before the turn of the 20th century. The Eaton Hall Railway, of 1895, was a private 15 inch gauge line serving the Duke of Westminster's estate in Cheshire. In the United Kingdom the narrow gauge had been generally seen as of need only to mines and quarries.

The more recent history of narrow gauge lines begins not in England but in France. In the late 19th century Paul Decauville inherited an agricultural machinery business and devised a system of 60 cm gauge portable light railway for use on farms. Easily transportable, this was designed to be laid by local labour without the need to use any specialized equipment. German firms also seized on this idea, and agricultural railways were laid not only in their home countries but also extensively in the French and German colonies serving a variety of agricultural concerns. There was also, for example, an extensive network of agricultural narrow gauge railways on the Somme, in France, prior to World War I.

The advantage of portable track was that it could be laid, and moved if necessary, by the existing farm labour. However, the lighter the track used the lighter loads that it could carry. The lightest rail in common use, by the time of World War I, was 9 lb. per yard. This, as the War Department (WD) was soon to discover, was acceptable for man or horse haulage but, if a locomotive was to be used, the 20 lb. per yard rail was required. This was much heavier. Experiments were carried out to try to design a light tractor which could stay on the lighter rail but with very little success.

The French and German armies, before World War I, were equipped with prefabricated light railway material to support their armies in the field. It was not until the British Army took over trenches formerly occupied by the French, together with their railway support, that it, too, realized the value and began to equip itself. The use of such lines to cross heavy ground and carry all the needs of the Army was well proven. After the end of the war large amounts of track, wagons and other equipment was sold cheaply as surplus to requirements and the Lincolnshire farm railways were able to reach their zenith.

Since the years of World War II, with the growth in road transport, rural roads have improved. This, together with increased costs of labour and costs of transhipment from one form of transport to another, has led to the disappearance of farm railways from the county's rural scene. Today articulated lorries reach every farmstead, and often, directly into the fields themselves.

This has led to an unusual present day feature in common with the landscapes of Lincolnshire and parts of the former front lines on the Western Front. Since the closure of the farm railways in Lincolnshire many farms have fence posts formed from cut lengths of rail. Farms in France and Belgium also have this, in both cases using rails from the same source.

The farm railways may have gone but potatoes are still grown in Lincolnshire. Here, on Porters Marsh at Grainthorpe in June 2002, they are growing to the left of the farm roadway. The latter was once the route of a railway on this farm, laid by Raymond Caudwell. *Author*

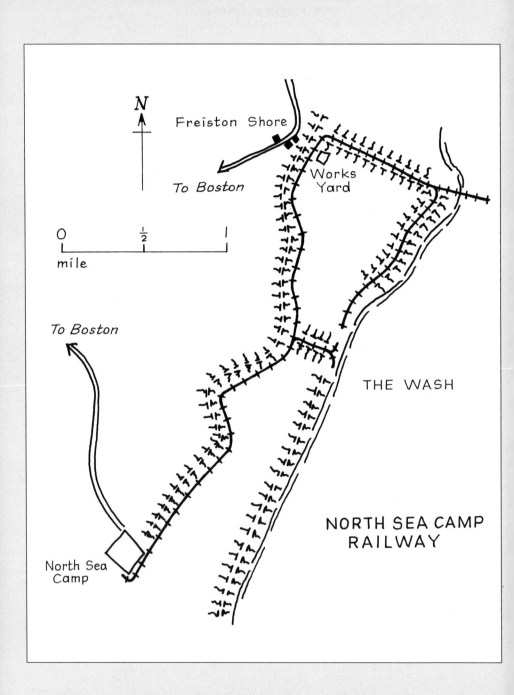

Chapter Three

Railways for Reclamation and Drainage

Narrow gauge railways had a role to play in both the reclaiming of land from the sea for agriculture and for the maintenance of the drains and waterways that ensured the land remained suitable for farming.

The North Sea Camp Railway

Near to the south-west corner of the Wash, immediately north of the point that the River Witham enters the sea, is North Sea Camp. This is now a prison but was first established as a Borstal in 1935. A Borstal was a detention centre for young men who would atone for their crimes by a process of hard work and education. It was seen as a punishment and this rather bleak and exposed location was certainly no holiday camp.

This was quite a contrast to the attitude of the mid-18th century visitors to the area who came to bathe and drink the seawater for the benefit of their health. Three miles to the north at Freiston Shore two hotels were opened to cater for them. When the railways came in the middle and late 19th century they took the visitors to Skegness and the days of the resort of Freiston Shore came to an end.

The first Borstal boys arrived at an open site and lived in tents. They built the huts they were to live in and cultivated the fields to provide much of their food. They also had the task of reclaiming around 600 acres of the foreshore from the sea to extend their agricultural holding. Both the reclamation and the farming activities were very much part of the regime at the Camp which provided for hard physical work and discipline.

The reclamation work comprised the construction of sea banks. For these soil was dumped using a 2 ft gauge railway. Lengths of temporary track were laid along which a tipper truck would be pushed manually to the place it was needed. This became the only prison railway in the country.

The weather was not the only hazard the inmates had to contend with. At the outer end of their work sites they were working below high tide level in an area that was inundated by the sea every day.

As work proceeded further from the Camp, to the north, the distances involved brought about the introduction of a 'main line' together with locomotives. This main line eventually extended from the camp northwards to Freiston Shore. From this temporary track would be laid to the various working sites. The locomotives were a fleet of six Lister diesels delivered at a variety of dates between 1939 and 1970 and all of which survive. Their details are given in *Table One* overleaf.

North Sea Camp. In 1985 the view from the sea bank with the tide in shows an excavator and an unidentifiable pile of material standing in the sea.   *Tony Wall*

North Sea Camp. With the tide out the material is revealed as a stock of narrow gauge rails and the route of the line used to maintain the banks. Few narrow gauge railways can have operated under such conditions.   *Tony Wall*

Table One
Lister Diesels used at North Sea Camp*

Works No.	Date Built	Notes
10994	1939	Privately owned in Derbyshire.
33650	1949	Privately owned in Gloucestershire.
33651	1949	Cosmetically restored and on display at the Prison Service College, Newbold Revel, Warwickshire.
51917	1960	Privately owned in Dorset.
55413	1967	Cosmetically restored and displayed at North Sea Camp until 2005. Now privately owned in Gloucestershire.
56371	1970	Privately owned in Gloucestershire. Believed to be the last to be constructed at the Dursley works.

* All had diesel engines and are 2 ft gauge

The sea banks were created with a base of interlocking blocks of concrete onto which the bank was built using silt from the tide washed foreshore. Silt was dug using an excavator loading into tip wagons which were then taken to the work site.

Land reclamation ceased with the completion of the last sea bank in 1979. From then on the use of the railway declined. By this time the inmates of the prison were farming a narrow strip of reclaimed land about three miles long. The railway was then used both for bank maintenance and to transport the workers from the prison to their work sites. For this latter use some crude four-wheel passenger 'carriages' were created from tip wagon chassis. This use soon ended with increasing Health and Safety requirements ruling that unsprung wagons with simple pin couplings and no brakes were too dangerous to use for this purpose.

At this time also the line had reached its greatest extent, about 2⅝ miles. The 'main' line ran northwards from the prison, at the foot of the seaward side of the earlier sea bank, to Freiston Shore, some 1¾ miles. At a point approximately half-way a second line ran along the top of a bank out to and along the seashore to one of the two work sites. At either end of this branch was a small shed for housing locomotives. There was a works depot at Frieston Shore where the line again ascended a sea bank to run out to the shore, then south along the top of the latest new bank.

From 1980 bank maintenance provided an intermittent use for sections of the line. As the sea banks had been pushed forward they became increasingly susceptible to erosion by the sea and needed repair from time to time. By the end of 1985 the decision was taken to close the railway and it was dismantled.

The locomotives went into store and panels of track were piled up at strategic points along the sea banks. Two of the locomotives and some of the tipper wagons were cosmetically restored and placed on display: locomotive No. 55413 and two wagons at North Sea Camp and No. 33651 with three wagons at the Prison Service College.

The Camp became an adult prison in 1988. At that time the then Governor proposed that the railway could be restored. Inmates would acquire skills in the manufacture, maintenance and running of a light railway operating a public service along the sea bank. In the prison workshops a fleet of six carriages were built utilising tip truck chassis but the idea foundered. It was revived again in 2001 but, again, it came to nothing.

The equipment was sold in 26 lots on 16th March, 2005. Two locomotives, many lengths of track and spare parts were sold to other lines and private owners nationwide. The six carriages constructed in the late 1980s remained in the County, however, and are being used on the North Ings Farm Railway (*see Chapter Eight, North Ings Farm Railway*).

Reclamation ceased because it was no longer practical to keep out the sea. The point had been reached where the cost of repairing damage to the man made banks was no longer economic. Perhaps ironically, the sea has now been allowed to reclaim some of the land. A policy of 'planned retreat' has seen some banks breached to allow the sea to re-establish saltmarsh. The Wash is an important habitat for sea birds and the nature conservation interest is now more important than maintaining small areas of farmland.

North Sea Camp. In 1985, shortly before closure, a train of tip wagons has been brought from the foreshore with material for tipping to strengthen the sea bank. One of the line's Lister locomotives is at the head of the train.   *Tony Wall*

Lincolnshire River Board. Maintenance work on a drain alongside the northern edge of Lincoln's West Common, west of the A57, in the winter of 1967/68. The locomotive is a Ruston and Hornsby 13DL, Works No. 224311. This was the only locomotive owned, at that time, by the Welland and Nene River Authority. It was hired to the Lincolnshire River Board for a period after 1966. The view also encapsulates the character of these lines, with their temporary track. *Tim Hudson*

Land Drainage - The Lincolnshire River Board and The Welland River Board

The River Boards had the responsibility of maintaining rivers and drains in the County for the benefit of agriculture and for flood protection. Many of these are remote from roads and some substantial civil engineering works were often required to construct and maintain embankments. The Boards had been established in 1931, as the Witham and Steeping Rivers Catchment Board and the Welland Catchment Board respectively.

To help with this work the Boards had locomotives, skip wagons and panels of temporary track forming a peripatetic railway. This would be laid along the river banks from the site where work was taking place, linking with the nearest road or to a convenient point where a barge could moor. Trains would usually comprise up to eight tipper wagons.

The track and locomotives were all of 2 ft gauge and the locomotives were all by the Lincoln manufacturer Ruston & Hornsby. The Lincolnshire River Board equipment was kept and maintained at the River Board Depot at Southrey, on the banks of the River Witham. The Welland River Board had their depot at Little London in Spalding. The latter became the Welland and Nene River Authority in 1965.

Table Two
River Board Locomotives*

a. Lincolnshire River Board

No.	Works No.	Class	Date	Notes
1	178999	18/21	1936	Delivered new, sold for scrap 1964.
2	179000	18/21	1936	Delivered new, sold for scrap 1964.
	211585	20DL	1941	Hired 1947 to 1950 from T.W. Ward.
	211592	20DL	1941	Hired 1947 to (by) 1952 from T.W. Ward.
	202999	20DL	1941	Hired 1947 to (by) 1950 from T.W. Ward.
3	421432	LA	1959	Delivered new, donated to Museum of Lincolnshire Life, 1986.
4	431433	LA	1959	Delivered new, sold into private preservation, 1986.

b. Welland River Board

	224311	1943	13DL	Delivered new, loaned to Lincolnshire River Board from 1966. Sold in 1973 after return to Spalding.

* All were Ruston and Hornsby 4-wheel diesel.

The two locomotives delivered new in 1959 to the Lincolnshire River Board were sold by the Anglian Regional Water Authority, to whom the drainage responsibility had evolved, in 1986. No. 431432, was rescued for the Museum of Lincolnshire Life in Lincoln and is on view in the Museum. The other, No. 421433, is now at the North Ings Farm Railway at Dorrington (*see Chapter Eight*), and can be seen working there on open days.

Lincolnshire River Board. At the working site, again in the winter of 1967/1968, No. 224311 handles a train of six tipper wagons. Near to the locomotive is one of the Board's excavators, a Ruston Bucyrus, fleet No. LRB4, another product of Ruston's and, like the locomotive, made in Lincoln.   *Tim Hudson*

Chapter Four

Potato Railways: Rise and Decline

This Chapter opens with an explanation of some of the terms used in the text. Throughout this book the crop is referred to as potatoes. In Lincolnshire, however, the vernacular term, still in use today, is 'taates'.

Potatoes originally came from South America. It is popularly supposed that Sir Walter Raleigh was the first to introduce them in England. It was not until the growth of towns and the change from subsistence farming from around 1750 that they began to be grown in increasingly greater numbers. Cheap and filling, they were an ideal food for the poor in both town and country. By the end of the 19th century disease in potatoes was being eradicated and their cultivation methods being improved. Growing competition in grain from North America, Russia and the Argentine led to Lincolnshire farmers looking for alternative crops and they turned increasingly to potato growing. The Great Northern Railway, in particular, encouraged production campaigning to encourage farmers to make use of the advantages of the railway to get them to market.

The third link in the chain was the entrepreneurship of the farmers, especially A.H. Worth, George Caudwell and William Dennis, who went into potato production in a big way. These three men, together with their families, were the Peers of the Potato. The Caudwell family farmed at Dawsmere; Grainthorpe; Holbeach St Marks; Holbeach St Matthew; Marshchapel; North Somercotes; Tetney; and Weston. The Dennis estates were at Crowland; Deeping St Nicholas; Fosdyke; Frampton; Moulton; Nocton; and West Butterwick. The Worth family had land at Fleet; Havenhouse near Skegness; Holbeach St Matthew; and at Prickwillow, east of Ely. On all of these light railways were built. The Dennis family, in 1903, were known as 'the Potato Kings of Lincolnshire', and donated all the potatoes for the Coronation festivities for the poor, in London, in 1902. William Dennis had a saying, 'Plough deep, till the soil, plant good seed, manure liberally, but first get the water off your land'.

In the 1880s it was said that the man who farmed five acres of potatoes accounted for a person of some substance. By World War I farms upwards of 1,000 acres were not uncommon. There were many more of 100 to 400 acres and scores of growers with farms ranging from 10 to 100 acres. The small farm worked by hand evolved into larger holdings using machinery after scientific analysis of the soil. Productivity increased tenfold.

A variety of crops were grown on most farms in the early years of this century. This type of farming was known as a rotation, the main objective of which was to control weeds and spread the workload of men and horses. Also, since considerable numbers of livestock were kept, food crops for these animals were needed. Though artificial fertilisers were coming into use, the main source of manure was the droppings of the livestock, additional nitrogen being provided by the growth of legumes, clover, peas and beans. Fenland potato growers were well known for their lavish use of artificial fertilisers before this

The statue of William Dennis, 1841-1924, in front of the Town Hall at Kirton, near Boston. The relief panel to the left of the base records his work as a potato grower.   *Author*

became general elsewhere. In the very early days this was guano, dried bird droppings from South America, and later, superphosphate. Quantities used were considerable; commonly 10 to 15 cwt an acre, with some farmers saying 'may as well make a good job of it and apply the ton'.

Potatoes are grown from seed potatoes, small potatoes grown especially for the propagation of the next crop. A few weeks before planting they are laid out in wooden trays in a light, warm building called a chitting house. This is usually, in effect, a greenhouse. They will not be planted in the ground until they are chitted, that is, until they begin to sprout green shoots, or chits, as they are known. Early potatoes are planted in January and February with the main crop going in in March and April. In the early 20th century they were sown at 15 to 20 cwt to the acre.

Crops were harvested in the late summer and the autumn, but the demand for them was constant, hence storage was needed. Grain, for example, harvested in the late summer, was taken from the fields and built into stacks. The stack would be within or near to a yard in which a threshing machine, driven by a steam traction engine, could be used to separate the grain from the straw. Grain yields at this time were around 1 to 1½ tons per acre. Harvested in good weather, haulage from the fields in horse-drawn carts and wagons was no problem.

Potato harvesting took place in the late autumn and winter. Yields were of 8 to 10 tons per acre. In addition to the fertility of the soil, the lack of stones in fenland soil was a major advantage for potatoes. Stones damage the crop when harvested and thus reduce yields.

Once out of the ground, the potatoes would be stored in clamps, long piles of potatoes up to about six feet high, covered with straw and soil to protect them from the frost. From their distinctive appearance they were also known as 'graves'. Clamps took up a lot of space and were built in the fields at a point where they would be accessible throughout the winter. Potatoes were taken from these clamps, and riddled, that is sorted for size, and bagged up for sale before onward transhipment.

Writing in his book published in 1914, *Highways and Byways in Lincolnshire,* W.F. Rawnsley, in his visit to the Spalding area, said:

> From Deeping to Spalding the road is a typical fen road, three little inns and a few farm cottages and the occasional line of white smoke on the perfectly straight Peterborough and Boston railway is all there is to see save the crops or the long potato graves which are mostly by the roadside.
> The potato trade is a very large one. Every cart or wagon we passed at Easter time on the roads between Deeping and Kirton-in-Holland was loaded with sacks of potatoes, and all the farm hands were busy uncovering the pits and sorting the tubers. Donington and Kirton seem to be the centres of the trade, Kirton being the home of the man who is known as the potato king, and has many thousands of acres of fenland for this crop alone.

The credit for starting this agricultural transport revolution in Lincolnshire goes to George Caudwell, a farmer who lived at St Lambert's Hall, Weston, to the north-east of Spalding. He was a potato grower, experiencing the winter haulage problems previously referred to. He contacted Harry Peacock, one of the co-founders of the well-known Lincolnshire agricultural machinery firm of Peacock and Binnington, and asked for a quotation for the supply of a mile length of standard gauge railway on his land. Following discussions over the suitability of such a line, a German firm with great experience in the provision of narrow gauge lines in West Indian sugar plantations was asked to survey the site and suggested that narrow gauge would be most suitable. Mr Caudwell was not convinced, but was persuaded when the firm agreed to lay and equip the line for a one-year trial. If it were not a success they would make no charge. It was, however, a great success.

These deliberations have not been dated, but it was about 1909. The location of the line is similarly not known definitely, but was most probably part of that centred on Wraggmarsh House, at Weston, from where a branch ran southwards to St Lambert's Hall. The gauge of this line was two feet. This farm was purchased by Mr Caudwell in 1908 so does fit the known criteria well. Mr Caudwell went on to lay railways on several of his farms in the Spalding and Holbeach areas. His brother, Robert, introduced them onto his farms in the Grainthorpe area.

In addition to George Caudwell there were two other south Lincolnshire farmers who were starting to grow potatoes on an industrial scale. These were A.H. Worth of Fleet and William Dennis of Kirton. Both of these were quick to sieze the opportunity demonstrated of the value of this method of improving farm access. Mr Worth laid his own railway at Fleet in 1909 followed by William Dennis at Littleworth in 1910.

These men laid farm railways on many farms and not all were within Lincolnshire. A.H. Worth laid one on his Mettleham farm, at Prickwillow, near Ely.

After World War I large quantities of war-surplus track, engines and rolling stock were put on sale. The track was of 60 cm gauge, variously quoted as 1 ft 11¼ in., 1 ft 11½ in., or 2 ft gauge. Fenland farmers now seized their opportunity to provide better access to their land, and the heyday of the agricultural narrow gauge line now began.

As far as is known, two weights of rail were used: 20 lb. per yard on the more intensively worked lines with locomotives, such as Nocton, and 9 lb. per yard on the lighter, horse-worked lines, such as Grange Farm, Holbeach St Marks.

Few lines employed locomotives. The most extensive, those at Nocton, Fleet and Dawsmere, used them for most of their existence, others experimented with them, but the majority used horses. It made sense to do this as there were already horses on the farms, and the railway made their use more efficient. The 1935 Agricultural Returns recorded 39,843 horses on farms in the County, an average of three on every holding.

On the heavy land in winter, four horses may be needed to haul one cart loaded with five tons of potatoes out of the fields. Using the railway, on some farms with no gradients, one horse could haul up to six trucks loaded with 10 tons of produce. Another big advantage was that as speeds were so low, certainly on the horse lines, minimal maintenance was required. In their latter years, tractors were used to pull the trucks before replacing the railways completely.

Farmers large and small utilised railways. The most prominent potato producer and the greatest user of railways was the firm of W. Dennis & Sons who owned large estates at Nocton, 8,000 acres, Deeping St Nicholas, 2,000 acres, and in the Kirton area, 2,000 acres. Eventually they were to operate over 30 miles of line, 22 miles on their Nocton estate alone. At the other end of the scale were the lines serving small farms, several of them of less than one mile in length.

Most lines ended adjacent to a hard-surfaced public road at which point a dock or shed would be built to facilitate transfer of the produce into carts or lorries for onward transhipment. A few also ran to adjacent main railway lines where the goods could be transferred to and from railway wagons. In three cases, the Wraggmarsh House system at Weston and at West Butterwick and at Alkborough, they ran to navigable rivers.

Once laid, they tended to become a permanent feature because, although they could be moved around, and some were, it was a major operation. Also, although laid for use in the winter months, once down, most were then used all year round.

It has not always proved easy to estimate the true total mileage of railways on some individual farms. The information has been taken from a number of sources. These include written references, maps and plans together with a great deal of oral history. Where there is, or was, significant oral or written history, for example, at Nocton or North Somercotes, then extensive mileages have been revealed. Where such information has been limited it may well be that the true extent will have been, in some cases, under-represented. The totals will, therefore, represent the best known information in each case.

In total in Lincolnshire, in this book, there were over 140 miles of track in 50 different locations. The high point was the late 1920s when 128 miles were in operation at least in 35 locations. The first closure came in the late 1920s when Dennis's removed 2¼ miles at Littleworth, followed by two other small lines in the 1930s. On the outbreak of World War II, however, most were still in operation.

The years 1939 to 1945 saw a radical change in British agriculture. The need to produce the maximum amount of home grown food to reduce imports, together with the loss of skilled landworkers to the armed forces, required greater efficiency. This was brought about largely by mechanisation, and the horses that worked on almost every farm in 1939 were largely replaced with tractors by 1945. Many miles of concrete and stone farm roads were constructed to enable vehicles to move easily and the need for the railways fell, around half of them closing during this time. Mechanisation proceeded after the war, and in a few short years the day of the agricultural railway was over.

In 1945, the railways were being used at least at 24 locations. After the end of 1950 only five remained. After the end of 1955 only that at Nocton remained to soldier on for a few years longer. Most of this was to be closed in 1960, although one last vestige remained in use until 1969.

Today there is very little to be seen of these once-busy transport systems. Roadways have replaced many of them. There are no significant earthworks to mark their route. Almost the only remnants are occasional loading docks or goods sheds, fast being removed themselves. Farmers being thrifty people, lengths of rusting rail can be found in farmyards, now being used as supports or fence posts. Even these are becoming rare. The last years of the 20th century saw further dramatic changes to agriculture in the County. Mixed farming is now very rare,

Kirton station was on the former East Lincolnshire line between Spalding and Boston. Alongside the station William Dennis built a potato warehouse from where, among other farms, potatoes from Manor Farm at Frampton and Lammings Marsh Farm at Fosdyke would have been dispatched. The rail siding side of the warehouse is seen here in July 2002, shortly before demolition in 2004.   *Author*

the County is now almost all arable. Crops do not demand secure fencing as animals do and with the drastic reduction in the need for fencing the rail fence posts are no longer needed. The railways live on now mainly only in the memories of retired farmworkers, and almost without exception, in the memories of adults who used to play on them in their childhood. What can still be seen, however, are fields of potatoes and the County is still known for their very high quality.

Dennis Estates, Deeping St Nicholas. The potato warehouse at Littleworth station. This photograph was taken in 2002. A similar view in 1916 can be seen on page 128.   *Author*

Chapter Five

The Farm Railways Described

1. Flatts Farm, Alkborough

This farm had the distinction of being the most north-westerly in Lincolnshire. It is sited on a narrow stretch of low-lying land between the escarpment upon which Alkborough village sits and the confluence of the River Trent and the River Ouse. The two rivers combine here to form the River Humber. This was one of the farms that turned to the rivers to solve their transport problem.

The rivers here have been a transport highway for centuries, as they still are today. Many of the industries which grew up along the Lincolnshire bank of the Humber took full advantage of it. Brickworks, cement works and chalk quarries were established here, all linked to the river by a light railway. The only farm railway to do so was that at Flatts Farm.

The River Humber is tidal. As the tide falls banks of mud are exposed. The traditional boats using the river, Humber Keels and Sloops, were flat-bottomed and would beach themselves at high tide. A period of, sometimes, frenzied activity would then see the boat loaded or unloaded and allow it to refloat at the next high tide.

The Flatts Farm railway was very short, only a quarter of a mile. It ran from the farm buildings in a north-westerly direction to the bank of the Humber. It was built approximately in the 1930s and the date it was last used is not known. Horse-worked, it carried potatoes and carrots outwards and coal inwards. The 1937 *Kelly's Directory* recorded the farmer here as James Allenby.

2. Sawcliffe Farm, Roxby

A very rare exception in Lincolnshire, a farm railway not on fen or marsh. Sawcliffe farm, farmed in 1937 by Frank Revitt, is situated on the Lincoln Cliff.

The Lincoln Cliff is an escarpment that runs north and south through much of the western part of the County. To the north of Lincoln it is known as the Cliff and to the south, the Heath. The steep scarp slope forms the western edge, here rising steeply some 150 feet. Sawcliffe Farm is sited a little back from the top edge of the escarpment, on the 250 ft contour. Half a mile to the west, and 150 feet below, is the route of the North Lindsey Light Railway that opened in 1906. It was to link the farm with a siding on this railway that the line was built.

The line is shown on a map relating to a lease of land for ironstone working dated 12th September, 1923. On this, it runs for almost three-quarters of a mile south-west from the farm to the present day A1077 between Scunthorpe and Roxby. Here there was a level crossing and the line turned due west to run down the steep face of the hillside. Alongside the railway a siding is shown, serving not only the farm but also a brickworks, shown in 1923 as 'Disused'. After running side by side for a short distance the farm railway ran into a building, marked as 'Farm Shed'.

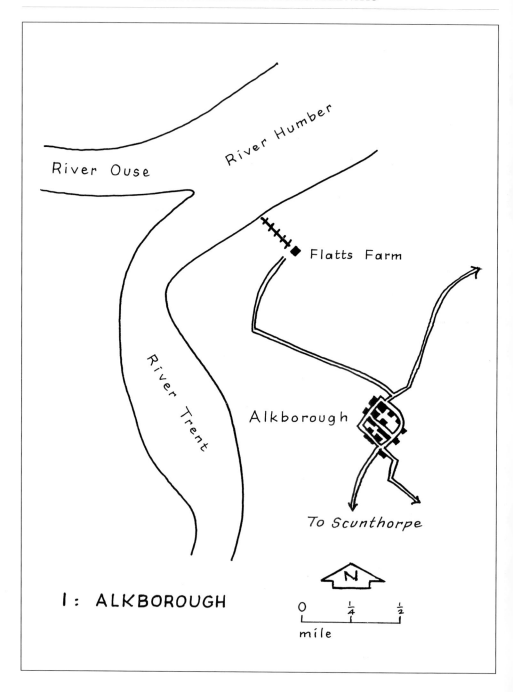

River Ouse

River Humber

Flatts Farm

River Trent

Alkborough

To Scunthorpe

N

1: ALKBOROUGH

0   ¼   ½

mile

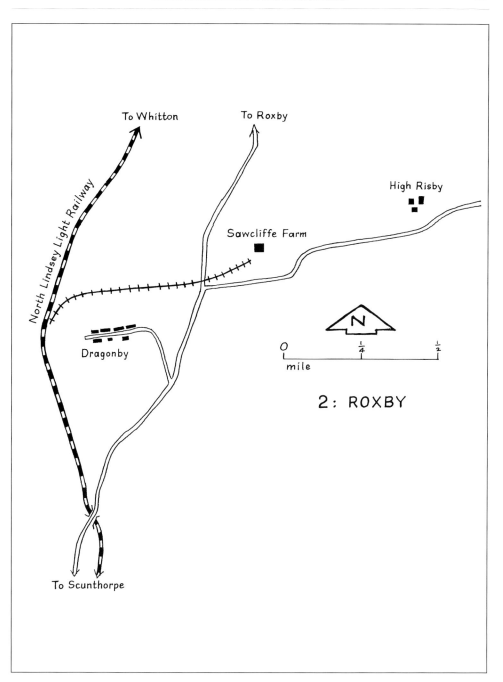

2: ROXBY

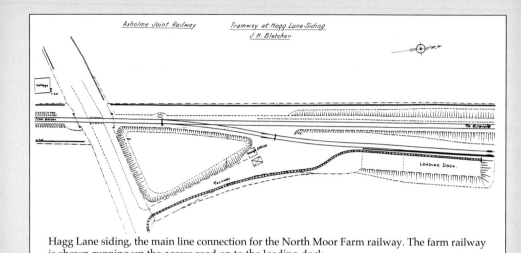

Hagg Lane siding, the main line connection for the North Moor Farm railway. The farm railway is shown running up the access road on to the loading dock.

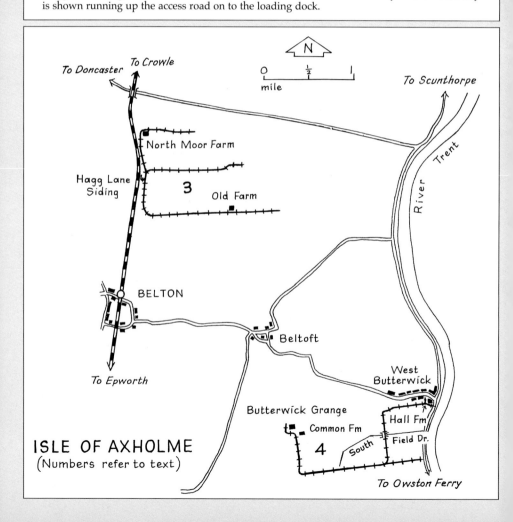

ISLE OF AXHOLME
(Numbers refer to text)

3. North Moor Farm, Belton

North Moor Farm, Belton, and Red House Farm near Thorne, just over the County boundary in South Yorkshire, were two of the farms owned by Mr John Henry Bletcher. In the late 19th century, Mr Bletcher was Chairman of the Isle of Axholme Light Railway, later the Axholme Joint Railway, linking Haxey with Goole, which opened throughout on 2nd January, 1905. This demonstrates an interest in railways which, he being an astute farmer, led to the construction of light railways on his two local farms, just after the Great War.

North Moor Farm lay alongside the Axholme Joint Railway and a siding, Hagg Lane Siding, was provided to serve the farms in the area. Here, in 1910, a loading dock was provided for Mr Bletcher's use. The Agreement for this, dated 21st March, 1910, included the following condition:

> In consideration of your providing a loading dock for the accommodation of five wagons at Hagg Lane Siding near to Belton, I the undersigned John Henry Bletcher of Worlaby in the County of Lincoln hereby undertake and agree that in the event of the total amount of traffic received at or forwarded by me after the completion of the said Loading Dock from the said Siding in any year or part of year ending the 31st day of December being received and forwarded at the rate of less than 2,500 tons per annum I will pay to you in respect of such year or part of a year as the case may be a yearly sum equal to 6% on the cost of the said Loading Dock (not exceeding £200) as certified by your Engineer and so in proportion for any less time than a year. Provided that this undertaking shall operate so long only as I shall occupy or continue tenant of the North Moor Farm.

Mr Bletcher was obviously confident of the need for and the success of the loading dock in serving the needs of the farm.

After World War I the use of the dock was further enhanced by the laying of a farm railway. A quantity of Army surplus 2 ft gauge track was purchased and by 1920 1¼ miles of it was laid on North Moor Farm, from Hagg Lane Siding on the Axholme Joint Railway, due east into the fields, and north to North Moor Farm. It was then extended eastwards from North Moor Farm, and south and east from Hagg Lane Siding to a point east of Old Farm, forming the shape of a capital letter E, with a total length of some three miles. In addition, lengths of track were kept at the end of the central stroke of the 'E' to be temporarily laid into the fields wherever needed.

The line was always horse-worked, the poor state of some of the second-hand track with its rusty metal sleepers precluding the use of a locomotive. For the opening, a number of four-wheel flat trucks, Army-surplus, were provided. Sides were built onto these by farm labour. Towards the end of its days, additional second-hand trucks were purchased from another, recently closed line, although which one is not known.

At Hagg Lane, the line ran up onto the dock from which produce was transhipped into, and out of, railway wagons. Crops of potatoes, peas and carrots were sent out, and fertiliser and seed potatoes were received.

In his book *The Axholme Joint Railway* (Oakwood Press, 1994) Colin Judge records that:

> In 1937, Charlie Arrand and Walter Powell used to work loading potatoes into trucks which were nicknamed 'Jubilee' trucks. The horses would then be harnessed to them by

roping across the length of the wagon to the back of the truck and not the fronts, this avoided them being pulled sideways off the uneven trackwork. Only two trucks were pulled at any one time and the horses uncannily knew which side of the track to walk so as to avoid walking over the points. The main line siding usually had five 8-ton open wagons and these were normally filled during the day. A porter from Belton station used to attend when the wagons were ready to be picked up.

From this some useful statistics can be derived. The normal daily output in the potato season was a total of 40 tons. Based on the experience of farms elsewhere in the County this would represent around 30 narrow gauge wagon loads a day.

A further point of interest is the reference to the trucks being known as 'Jubilee' trucks. The only Royal Jubilee in the inter-war years was that of King George V who celebrated 25 years on the throne in 1935. Perhaps this indicates that some trucks were acquired in that year.

After World War II, the line's use decreased with each passing year, and in about 1953 was dispensed with. Track which was still usable was sold to the British Moss Peat Co. for use on its narrow gauge lines on Thorne, Goole and Hatfield Moors. Some was passed on to the Lincolnshire Coast Light Railway (*see Chapter Eight*) to be cannibalised for spare parts.

Although outside the geographical limits of this book, the Bletcher's other line, at Red House Farm, deserves mention if only for the unique method adopted to reach its nearest railway siding, at Maud's Bridge, between Crowle and Thorne. The Stainforth & Keadby Canal forced the light railway to terminate on the opposite bank to the siding so a purpose made dray was built, on to which the wagons ran from a dock. A horse would then take the dray on, by road.

4. Hall Farm and Common Farm, West Butterwick

The Butterwick Estate was served by a light railway running in an indirect route from Butterwick Grange, via Common Farm, on Butterwick Common, to Hall Farm and the River Trent in West Butterwick village. The date it was laid is not known. Sale particulars of the Estate in 1911 make no reference to it, but it did exist before 1925.

It was built by the tenants, Dennis & Godfrey Ltd, the Dennis half being W. Dennis & Sons who made so much use of these railways countywide. The gauge is believed to have been two feet. The 'main' line, 2½ miles long, was Butterwick Grange to Hall Farm, with two sidings, one at Common Farm to a crewyard, and one to a loading dock in Hall Farm yard. There was also a short branch about 600 yards long, from Hall Farm to the bank of the River Trent, which crossed the Owston Ferry road by a level crossing. At the river's edge it ran up onto a small loading dock.

The line was horse-worked, and there were about 12 four-wheeled flat trucks with head and tailboards. On this farm they were referred to as 'trams', and the man who worked the horse the 'tramsman'. Some of these trams had a horizontal brake wheel; the brake was needed at a point where the line rose and fell to cross the South Field Drain. On the descent the brake would be applied to keep the chain connecting the trams to the horse taut to stop them running into him.

One horse was used regularly. Possessing the intelligence of his breed, he knew his job. Even in the direst ground conditions he knew where to step to keep his footing. If the tramsman was kept busy loading carts at a terminus, the horse could be harnessed to the empty trams and sent off on his own, safe in the knowledge that he would plod steadily back to the point they were needed. The regular load was five tons on three trams: 33 cwt on two and 34 cwt on the other. The docks, built to take three trams, were approached by a gradient which enabled only one tram at a time to be positioned. The horse pulled each one up to rest gently against its neighbour without being stopped. The tram was then immobilised with a 'sprag' under a wheel.

In the early years of this century the River Trent played a much greater part in the life of riverside communities than it does today. It was a highway along which boats passed carrying goods and passengers, tying up wherever there was call. At West Butterwick potatoes, grain and sugar beet were taken away, and seeds, fertiliser and cattle food were brought in, hence the branch to the bank. Boats were loaded and unloaded by hand, across narrow planks which bent under the weight of heavy bags carried on sweating backs, or pushed in barrows. There was a knack to this, the unwary being pitched, with his load, into the water.

To get the maximum use of the line, wherever possible potato clamps and haystacks were built close by. Cattle crewyards at Common Farm and Hall Farm were also adjacent to it. At Hall Farm the line ended inside a building used as a granary and bag store, and the trams were housed here overnight.

In 1925 the Estate was again sold. Hall Farm was purchased by Mr J. Godfrey, one of the former tenants, and Common Farm by Sir Frederick Hiam. The former did not want to use the line, the fields were all within easy reach of the

Hall Farm, West Butterwick. The route of the line in 1986 with Hall Farm in the background.
Author

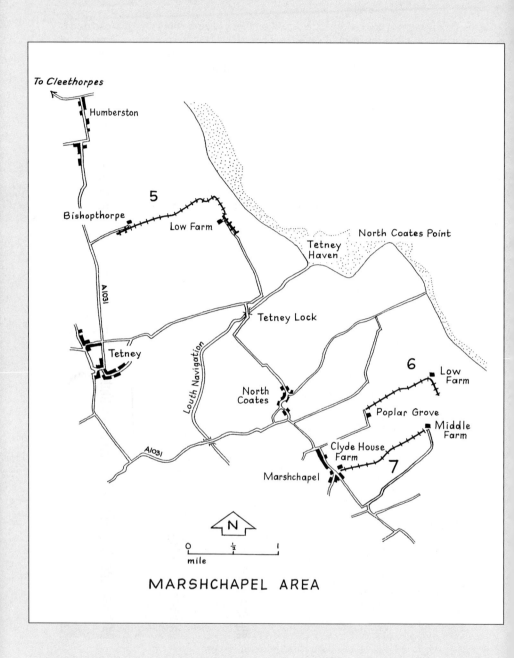

To Cleethorpes

Humberston

5

Bishopthorpe

Low Farm

North Coates Point

Tetney Haven

A1031

Tetney Lock

Tetney

Louth Navigation

6

Low Farm

North Coates

Poplar Grove

Middle Farm

A1031

Clyde House Farm

7

Marshchapel

N

0 ½ 1
mile

MARSHCHAPEL AREA

farmyard, but it was still needed on the latter. The solution was to close down the one mile section running west and south of Hall Farm, and to construct a new length, almost half a mile long, running eastwards from the existing route to terminate adjacent to the Owston Ferry road further south from the village. At this new terminus, a small corrugated-iron shed was built to house the trams, together with a short siding onto a loading dock.

In 1939 Common Farm was again sold. In the sale particulars appeared the following; 'The tramway and the tramshed (but not the trolleys etc.) are included in the sale and will be found to be a great labour saving asset'. The buyer, Mr 'Sammy' Moore, immediately decided to replace the line with a concrete road. The final duty of horse and line was to help build this new road. A number of skip trucks were purchased, the concrete mixed alongside the road, and, loaded into these, taken along the rails to be progressively tipped. On the completion of this task the light railway and its equipment were sold for scrap. No trace remains of it today.

5. Bishopthorpe, Tetney

Robert Caudwell, one of the Caudwell brothers, farmed at Tetney, Marshchapel and North Somercotes. He laid 2⅗ miles of track to serve his Bishopthorpe and Low Farms at Tetney. The date it was built is not known, but many sidings served large wooden sheds used as storage buildings which were purchased as Army surplus after World War I. It may be, therefore, that the railway was set up from the same source. If so, it could be expected to be 2 ft gauge although the one wagon which survived on this farm was of 2 ft 6 in. gauge (*see Appendix Two*).

Bishopthorpe Farm, Tetney. The wagon discovered on this farm in 1987 in the position it languished with other surplus farm equipment.   *Author*

The line was first recorded on the 1932 1:10,560 OS map. There were a number of flat four-wheel trucks, similar in appearance to those used at Wraggmarsh House at Weston.

The railway survived World War II, although it is believed to have been little used in its final years. It was replaced by a farm road by 1949, the rails being used for other purposes around the farm.

6. Low Farm, Marshchapel

This was probably the shortest-lived of all potato railways, and one of three built by Robert Caudwell on his Marsh Farms. It ran from Low Farm to the road adjacent to Poplar Grove Farm. The gauge was 2 feet, and 1¼ miles of track was laid by farm labour in 1938. This may well have been the very last farm railway laid in Lincolnshire. Horse-worked, it was closed and dismantled in 1943.

7. Clyde House Farm, Marshchapel

S.S. Mossop, a Holbeach lawyer, purchased this 330-acre farm in 1935. It is believed that no light railway existed on the farm at this time and that Mr Mossop was the builder, bringing the idea with him from an area that was successfully operating on so many farms there. Certainly, the farm records include correspondence dated 22nd July, 1935 confirming the sale of land from an adjacent farm in the village to enable the construction of a light railway dock adjacent to a road. The line was, therefore, one of the last built in the County. The gauge is not known.

The farm records also include a letter dated 24th March, 1946 to Messrs Christian and Dobbs, of Long Sutton (*see Appendix Three*).

> Referring to my letter of the 16 inst, my son has come to the conclusion that certainly for another year he can do without any additional light railway.

This may be taken to indicate that the firm were the suppliers of the equipment for the line, as they had been to Lighthouse Farm at Sutton Bridge.

The line was horse-worked. Part of its route is uncertain, but it is known that it ran from the yard at Clyde House Farm at least halfway to Middle Farm, if not all the way, a total distance of 1¼ miles. Its main use was for the transport of potatoes.

It was short-lived. The onset of mechanization leads the present owner to believe that it must have been removed about 1946.

This is one of the lines on which people have fond memories of playing as a child. Here, on a Sunday, all the wagons would be at the farmyard. On days when the wind was suitable a makeshift sail would propel a wagon out onto the Marsh. Children being what they were would abandon the wagon at the end and walk back for another, resulting, on the Monday morning, with the wagons being in the wrong place for the start of the day's work.

8. Caudwell's Farms, Grainthorpe and North Somercotes

This was another of Robert Caudwell's estates in this area. It was on land, in the parishes of both Grainthorpe and North Somercotes, lying between the villages and the sea, a distance of two miles. The farms covered an area of around three square miles. A previous owner, Henry Pye, a Louth solicitor, reclaimed 320 acres of saltmarsh along the shore here from the sea. He bought the land in 1843. In an attempt to improve access for both materials and farm produce, Pye dug a drainage channel that included a cut from the sea providing access for boats.

Certainly by the end of World War I Robert Caudwell was not using the sea access. In about 1924, he built several miles of narrow gauge railway line to open up access within the estate. This was to provide access to the long established existing roads running between the villages. The line linked the farmsteads on the Marsh with almost all of the fields. The total mileage appears to have been about 11½ miles. However, although the main links between the roads and the farms were permanent, the links with individual fields were often not so. Lengths of track would be laid and used for a season or two and then moved. They might be subsequently reinstated; it would be dependent upon the crops being grown at any particular time.

The lines were laid and moved using his own farm labour force. The track was of 18 ft lengths of 9 lb. per yard rail spiked to wooden sleepers. Permanent track linked the three main termini, Marsh Grange, The Holmes and Range End. These were the main links with the outside world into which seeds and fertilizer arrived and from where produce was taken away. *En route*, the lines connected with Pyes Farm, Range Farm, Rookery Farm, Sea Farm and one with the romantic name of Cape Horn. The latter is, perhaps, an indication of what the weather here can be at times. With the winter wind in the east, bringing weather systems in from Russia, it can be very cold. Pyes Farm was originally called Home Farm, but the name was changed to avoid confusion with The Holmes. There was no farmstead at Range End. It was simply a convenient point where lorries could gain access direct from the main road. Another similar location was Haxby's Field. Here was a convenient road link but this was used generally for the farm's internal needs.

The centre of operations for the farm and the railway, where trucks were stored and maintained, potatoes stored, animal food milled and peas vined, was The Holmes. This was a collection of cottages and a variety of sheds, known locally then, as it is today, as 'Tin Town'.

The line was believed to have been about 2 ft 6 in. gauge. It was horse-worked, and equipped with a mixture of around 50 small flat and plank-sided trucks. These were usually operated in rakes of six. In addition, some iron tipping trucks were used to carry gravel from a small quarry near to The Holmes for use in road making and repair. Because of a slight gradient between Range End and Range Farm some additional brake trucks were kept at the latter to help with the load on the downward gradient.

Fully loaded, a horse could cope with a load of up to 12 tons. It was used mainly for potatoes but grain, feed for cattle, horses and pigs, and coal, coke and peas were also carried.

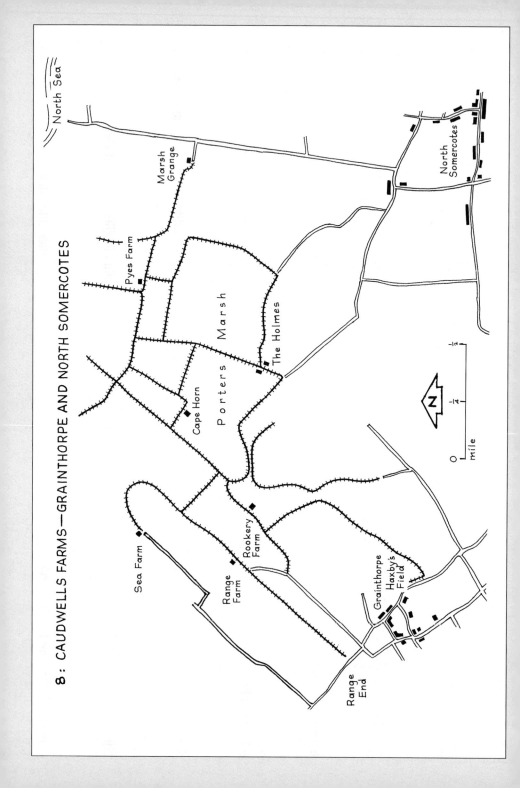

8: CAUDWELLS FARMS—GRAINTHORPE AND NORTH SOMERCOTES

North Sea

Marsh Grange

Pyes Farm

Porters Marsh

Cape Horn

The Holmes

North Somercotes

Sea Farm

Range Farm

Rookery Farm

Range End

Grainthorpe

Haxby's Field

N

mile
0   ¼   ½

Caudwell's Farm, North Somercotes. The former loading dock at Marsh Grange Farm, North Somercotes, in 2002.   *Author*

Caudwell's Farm, North Somercotes. Henry Pye improved Grainthorpe Haven after he reclaimed the saltmarsh from the sea after 1843. The Humber keels and sloops that would have brought produce in and out were flat-bottomed so that they could be beached, when necessary, at low tide.   *Author*

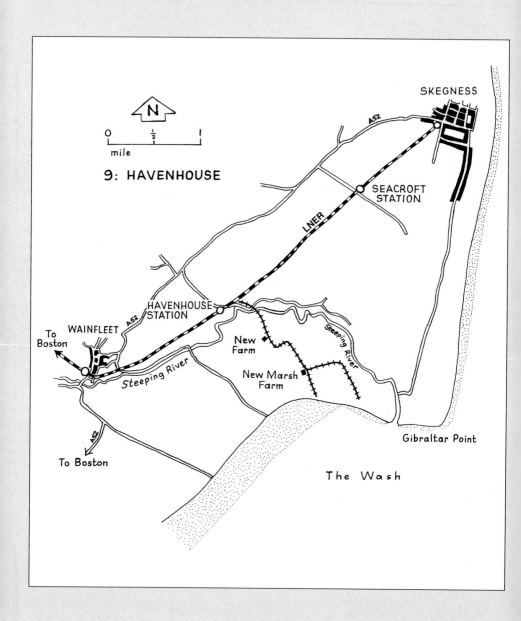

N

0   ½   1
mile

9: HAVENHOUSE

SKEGNESS

A52

SEACROFT
STATION

LNER

HAVENHOUSE
STATION

WAINFLEET

To
Boston

A52

Steeping River

New
Farm

New Marsh
Farm

Steeping River

Gibraltar Point

A52

To Boston

The Wash

Robert Caudwell was considered to be an innovative farmer and was the first to grow potatoes on a large scale in this part of Lincolnshire. He also built his own telephone system in the early 1930s, linking his home at Grainthorpe House with the outlying farms.

After harvesting, the potatoes were put in clamps at a convenient point where they could be easily reached by temporary sidings. They could then be sorted at the site, from where they were taken in bags to a rail served store at Pyes Farm where they could be kept under cover. From here, they were carried to Marsh Grange where there was a loading dock for transfer to lorries. This was 115 feet long and seven feet wide. A horse would pull trucks up on to this one at a time. Pig potatoes, that is, those too small, or damaged, making them unsuitable for human consumption, were taken to Marsh Grange where there was a steamer to render them suitable as pig food. At the end of the line at Marsh Grange there was also a turntable. Given that no locomotives used the line it is difficult to determine why one was needed.

After the Smith's Crisps factory opened in Lincoln in 1938 special varieties of potatoes were also grown for them. Their lorries would collect the potatoes from Range End to where they were delivered by the farm railway. Problems were experienced here because the lack of sidings. As space was limited for lorries to stand by the line and, at times, there were three lorries to fill, when a rake of trucks was unloaded they were unceremoniously run off the end of the track to make room for the next rake. Re-railing was a simple matter as two men could manhandle them back on the line one at a time when empty.

The railway went out of use in 1950, by which time the system appears to have been reduced to the stretch from Pyes Farm to The Holmes, and the Cape Horn branch. The only surviving remnant is the Marsh Grange dock. The rails were cut up for use as fence posts, one 18 ft rail making, very conveniently, three 6 ft fence posts. Some of these still survive on the Marsh. In addition, spikes for holding the rails down also turn up occasionally on the farm roadways.

9. New Marsh Farm, Havenhouse

A major landowner in the parish of Wainfleet St Mary, in which the railway ran, was T.H. Worth, one of the farming family who had established their own light railway at Fleet, near Holbeach, in 1909. This accounts for this line being established here.

In the spring of 1927 three miles of 2 ft gauge track was laid to serve the fields on New Farm and New Marsh Farms, together a total of 800 acres. The rail sections were 16 ft 6 in. long laid on 4 ft pressure-creosoted wooden sleepers spaced at 3 ft intervals. Metal spreaders bolted to the bottom of the rails allowed slight adjustments to be made to the gauge. Sections were joined by fishplates and the whole was fastened to the sleepers by dog spikes.

The route ran from the fields to the farmyards and onto Havenhouse station on the branch line between Wainfleet and Skegness. To reach the station the Steeping River was crossed by a 60 ft-span steel bridge. In the station yard the

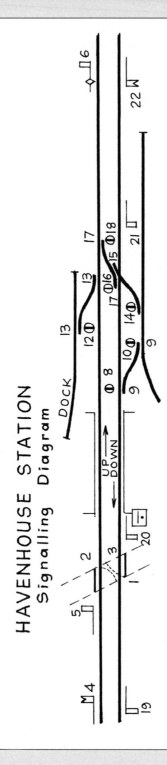

The siding and dock on the up side of the line were provided in 1928 for the railway serving New Marsh Farm.

rails were lifted onto a dock alongside a standard gauge siding to allow for direct transfer of goods between the two systems. This dock and the siding serving it, were operating from 1928 and it, therefore, seems likely that they were provided specifically for the narrow gauge railway.

To work the line a 20 hp Simplex locomotive, Motor Rail Works No. 4080, weighing 2½ tons, with a Dorman petrol engine was acquired. It was ordered by A.H. Worth of Holbeach and dispatched to T.H. Worth at Havenhouse station on 11th June, 1927. In operation, the maximum load it could haul on the line was 15 tons.

The traffic was mainly potatoes, hay, corn and straw bales outwards, and from the station 200 tons of seed potatoes from Scotland annually, and artificial manure dispatched originally from Kings Lynn, in Norfolk.

The line was in regular use until its replacement by tractors in 1948 or 1949. The track was then removed. William Greetham & Son purchased the locomotive for use in their Skegness Brickworks from where it was withdrawn from service about 1962. A similar engine survives, awaiting restoration, at the Lincolnshire Coast Light Railway at Winthorpe.

The line was referred to in Alf Ludlum's book *Railways to Skegness* (Oakwood Press, 1997). This, in the section on Havenhouse station, includes the following:

Other farming companies in the area were C.W. Parker and Worth Farms. The latter ran a 2 ft gauge light railway over three miles of track running between fields and crossing the River Steeping by a 60 ft span steel bridge, then following the river to Havenhouse station. Here a siding brought the light railway up to the level of the standard gauge wagon bottoms. The line was laid with rails 5.5 yards in length, laid at 3 ft spaces on 4 ft long pressure creosoted sleepers. Metal spreaders were bolted to the bottoms of the rails; these had a slight adjustment. Each section was joined by fishplates and the whole secured to the sleepers with dog spikes; a Dorman Simplex petrol driven engine was driven by Albert Miller and was capable of pulling 15 tons in dry conditions. The light railway transported potatoes, corn, hay and straw bales to the station returning with 200 tons per annum of seed potatoes and artificial manure from Kings Lynn.

10. Nocton Estate Light Railway

The Nocton Estate Railway was to become the largest and longest-lived agricultural narrow gauge railway in the county, if not the country, and is the one of which the most remains to be seen.

In 1919 W. Dennis & Sons established their Nocton estate of 7,800 acres. This included 3,700 acres on Potterhanworth, Nocton and Dunston Fens, 1,750 acres on the Boulder Clay around Nocton and Dunston villages, 450 acres of woodland and 1,900 acres on the limestone Heath to the west. It was seven miles east to west and two miles north to south. They were successfully using a light railway on their estate at Deeping St Nicholas, and wanted the same at Nocton.

Negotiations were opened between Tom Dennis, for the Estate, and the Great Northern Railway, acting on behalf of the Great Northern & Great Eastern Joint Railway, in May 1919 over the provision of a siding to serve their needs. This was to be at Nocton, but when the cost was estimated to be £2,281 to the Estate

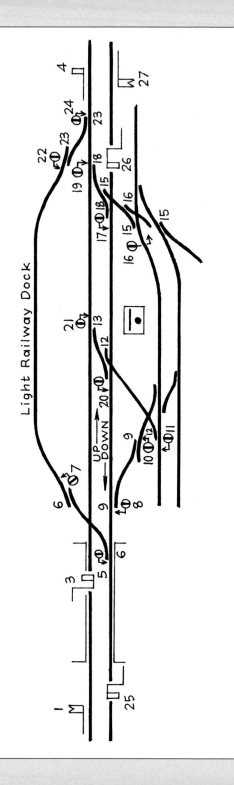

NOCTON STATION
Signalling Diagram

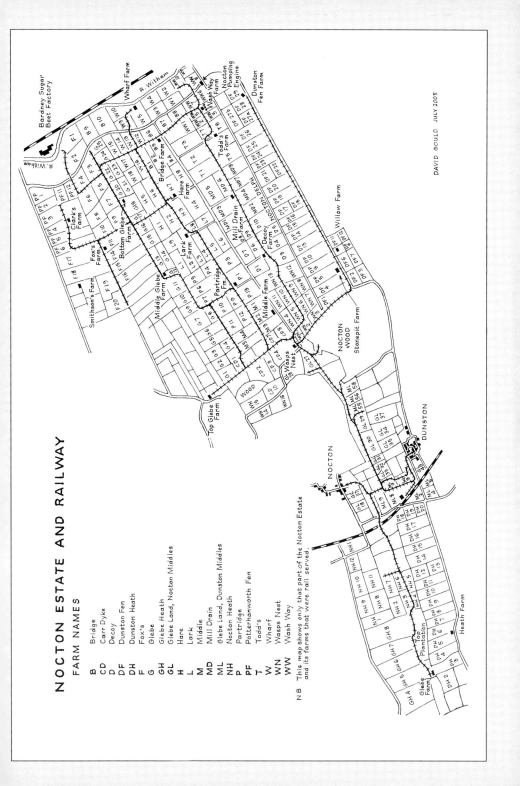

NOCTON ESTATE AND RAILWAY

FARM NAMES

B	Bridge
CD	Carr Dyke
D	Decoy
DF	Dunston Fen
DH	Dunston Heath
F	Fox's
G	Glebe
GH	Glebe Heath
GL	Glebe Land, Nocton Middles
H	Hare
L	Lark
M	Middle
MD	Mill Drain
ML	Glebe Land, Dunston Middles
NH	Nocton Heath
P	Partridge
PF	Potterhanworth Fen
T	Todd's
W	Wharf
WN	Wasps Nest
WW	Wash Way

N B   This map shows only that part of the Nocton Estate
       and its farms that were rail served.

DAVID GOULD JULY 2005

Nocton Estate. The Works photograph by John Fowler & Co. of Leeds of the 0-6-0 locomotive, Works No. 16991, built in 1926 for Dennis Estates for use at Nocton. It was said that it would haul up to 204 tons on the level and up to 50 tons up the gradient from Wasps Nest. At over 11 tons in weight it proved too heavy for the fenland tracks and tended to spread the rails on the higher ground.

Institute of Agricultural History

the alternative, at Bardney, was briefly considered. Here, however, the proposed light railway could not reach the station yard without a substantial bridge over the River Witham. The option of cartage over the existing road bridge was considered but ruled out, presumably because of the extra double handling that would be needed. A revised costing at Nocton, requiring a contribution of £1,666, was also not acceptable to the Estate. They argued that they would be bringing a considerable revenue to the railway and they were offering as their contribution the land for their siding. If this siding were not built then the railway company would have to provide an additional siding in its own goods yard for the traffic which would be at its own expense. The wrangling dragged on through the summer and into the next year, further exacerbated over the status of a footpath alongside the up line which people from Dunston used to reach the station. In June 1920 Dennis was pressing for urgent action. His men had started work on the light railway; in June he was arguing that the siding needed to be ready to receive traffic from the Fen in September and October; in July Dennis offered to put his own men on to construction work as he had a big staff of navvies at work who, once dispersed, he would not get back. These men were building the first four miles of 1 ft 11½ in. gauge tramway at Nocton on the heavy fenland east of Wasps Nest. The siding was built and eventually came into use at 10.00 am on 2nd February, 1921.

The centre of operations on the estate was adjacent to the main railway line between Lincoln and Sleaford, near Nocton and Dunston station. The Estate Manager at that time, a Major Webber, must have seen at first hand how effective narrow gauge railways were under terrible ground conditions during the Great War. It was he who inspired the purchase of a great quantity of 20 lb. per yard narrow gauge track and rolling stock from an Army-surplus depot at Arras, in France. The route was to reach almost 23 miles of single track. Taking the large number of sidings into account as well as lengths of temporary track for non-permanent use the total mileage amounted to around 35 miles. Although horse and man haulage of narrow gauge trucks would have taken place it is clear that from the start locomotive haulage was intended. This was the industrialization of agriculture on a major scale.

This was one of only two Lincolnshire farm railways to leave the Fenland. From Wasps Nest on the Fen edge it climbed up past Nocton village to the railhead, and on from there to the Heath and Glebe Farm. Five miles of the total route mileage were on this higher ground. From its lowest point adjacent to the River Witham in the east the line rose from 8 feet above sea level to 20 feet at Wasps Nest. It then climbed steeply to 50 feet in the next quarter of a mile. The railhead was at about 100 feet, the line rising again to an elevation of almost 160 feet on the approach to Glebe Farm.

Public roads were crossed on the level at six locations. Four of these were simple open crossings on the Bardney to Nocton road. Another was over Back Lane at Dunston to reach the Halls Yard Piggery. The sixth was a gated crossing over the B1198 Lincoln to Sleaford road. Their use was governed by an agreement between Dennis's and the County Council. In the 1930s a further short extension was proposed, through Nocton village northwards to Manor Farm. Preparation work involved the creation of gated gaps in roadside walls,

Nocton Estate. The Fowler locomotive was sold by the Estate to George Cohen and Sons of Leeds about 1930. Seen here at Burnhope in Durham, about 1936, where it had been used in the construction of a reservoir for Durham County Water Board. Still sporting its Nocton livery, the only apparent changes in its appearance are the substitution of a traction engine type chimney for its original American type spark arrestor, and a toolbox on top of the left-hand tank. Offered for sale in 1937, there were no customers and she was scrapped on site, at Burnhope, in 1938.

E.E. Smith

Nocton Estate. In the Nocton fields a train of potatoes starts its journey to the railhead. Simplex No. 5, Works No. MR3995, came second-hand, but Works reconditioned, in 1934. It was delivered without a cab; this was a local modification by the Estate workshops to protect the driver from the elements. A second seat for another crew member who had the job of opening gates, changing points and acting as shunter is seen here - the young man has his foot on it. *Redshaw Collection*

Nocton Estate. Simplex No. 4, Works No. MRT 2083, was delivered new to Nocton in 1923. It was stripped to the frame and used as a snowplough after 1936 in which guise it is seen here. It had a square frame instead of the usual bow. *Ron Redman*

Nocton Estate. MRT 1935 was one of the first locomotives at Nocton, where it carried the number 1, being delivered new in 1920. It was also the last to be used and sold to the Lincolnshire Coast Light Railway in 1969. It is seen here with the body given by its new owner on their line at Humberston, and now given the name *Nocton,* on 6th August, 1985. *Author*

and openings through both sides of a stone barn, but the scheme foundered when the County Council refused to sanction another level crossing, over the B1202 between two sharp bends because of the danger to road traffic.

Half a mile west of Nocton village, the Glebe Farm branch on to the Heath crossed the Lincoln to Sleaford railway on a bridge, shared with a farm roadway.

Such an extensive mileage and the number of trains running on it required a permanent staff of drivers, guards and platelayers. Away from the Estate Yard the Nocton track always appeared to be in a grass grown state. The reason was that weed control at that time involved the application of Sodium Chlorate which played havoc with metal track and sleepers.

The main product of the Estate was potatoes, but the need for crop rotation and the varying soils meant that a variety of produce, mainly potatoes, grain and sugar beet, was grown. In addition to arable farming, there were cattle, pigs and sheep.

The railway served every aspect of the operation. Almost every field on the Estate was reached so that produce could be harvested directly into trucks. When working in the larger fields, the track would be broken, a point inserted, and a short length of siding put in sufficient to hold about eight trucks, laid directly on to the surface. This left the through line clear for other trains. In the fields sugar beet would be loaded from the field into horse-drawn carts and tipped into the waiting railway wagons before being taken direct to the Bardney factory. Potatoes were taken in a cart to the nearest convenient point alongside a road or the railway and tipped to make a clamp or grave (*see Chapter Four*). In the grave the potatoes were protected from frost. The end was opened up as potatoes were required, then riddled, weighed and bagged in one hundredweight (50 kg) sacks. The full sacks were then loaded onto a wagon to be taken by rail to the estate yard.

The line ran through the greenhouse where potatoes were chitted and tomatoes grown, through the piggeries, from where muck was transported to be spread on the fields, and through the mill, where feed for the stock was prepared. At the railhead were the Estate workshops where all the machinery, including the railway vehicles, was maintained. Railway vehicles were also converted and adapted for new and changing uses here. The mill, greenhouse, workshop and an engine shed were all at the railhead, together with a dock for off-loading produce into lorries or into standard gauge railway wagons standing in the exchange siding. The siding was a loop off the up main line.

At its eastern extremity the Estate had the River Witham as its boundary. On the opposite bank, in 1927, the Bardney Sugar Beet Factory was built, incidentally, on land sold for the purpose by the Estate owners. Sugar beet from the Nocton Estate was carried to the factory by a mechanical grab running along a gantry over the river, the beet being picked up from a dump into which trucks were unloaded from sidings built for the purpose. The grab was also used to unload beet from barges in the river. After the railway closed the gantry was retained as a pipe bridge. Slurry from the processing at the factory was mixed with clean water and pumped over to filter beds on the Nocton bank. Here it was left to condition for sale to farmers the following year. This residue was used to improve the ph content of the fields in the fen.

Sugar Beet from the Estate went into the factory from the beginning. For the first Beet Season in 1927/28 Nocton supplied 7,104 tons, 9 per cent of the total

Nocton Estate. The prime reason for narrow gauge railways on Lincolnshire farms, the humble potato. Here on the fenland the clamp or grave of potatoes has been opened and five men are bagging them into sacks and loading them onto wagons among which are Nos. 34 and 35.

Redshaw Collection

Nocton Estate. In the fields on Dunston Fen potatoes are being riddled, bagged and weighed. These will have come direct from the field, delivered from the trailer at the far end with a tractor beyond. In the background Simplex No. 5 waits with a train to take them to the Estate Yard.

Redshaw Collection

processed. Beet continued to be supplied via the railway and the grab until 1951. *Table Three* includes the annual tonnage of beet from 1927 to 1951 produced by the Estate, carried by the light railway and crossing the river by the grab. Before unloading, the wagons crossed a weighbridge adjacent to the Fen road.

Table Three
Sugar Beet Delivered to the Bardney Factory by the Nocton Estate Railway, 1927 to 1951

Year	Tons	Light Railway Wagonloads
1927	7,104	2,154
1928	2,617	720
1929	2,829	744
1930	4,256	1,150
1931	3,063	906
1932	3,984	1,111
1933	5,675	1,574
1934	5,577	1,516
1935	4,594	1,189
1936	4,274	1,229
1937	2,710	797
1938	2,942	868
1939	4,191	1,274
1940	4,191	1,210
1941	3,422	980
1942	4,651	1,470
1943	3,540	1,118
1944	2,623	870
1945	3,506	1,092
1946	3,417	1,253
1947	1,715	511
1948	3,829	1,170
1949	3,924	1,082
1950	4,792	1,329
1951	3,341	934
Total	96,767	28,251

Other tasks performed by the railway were the transport of coal to the Nocton Pumping Engine which drained much of the Fen, before it was converted to electricity, and water to the cattle in the crew yards, and to the farms and cottages outside the village before piped water supplies were laid. The only supply these houses had was rainwater, and drainage dykes, so drinking water had to be taken to tanks provided at each one. The tanks were filled from a standpipe, south of Nocton where the railway crossed the Bridle Road from Nocton to Dunston and at Wasps Nest. A small stone quarry was also rail-connected. In later years, after the introduction of tractors, these were refuelled where they were working in the fields from specially converted tank wagons. The fuel was paraffin, and each vehicle had a trailer tank to hold its supply. The latter was always moved to a place alongside the light railway prior to the visit of the fuel train.

Nocton Estate. In November 1932 a train crosses the B road from Lincoln to Sleaford behind Ruston locomotive, Works No. 165365. This is clearly a posed photograph with the second gate closed to the train. The 3 ton lorry in the background carries a load typical of the period. Several of these lorries would be needed to replace a loaded train but they could not have got into the fields as the railway did. For use in their staff magazine Ruston's cropped the photograph to exclude the right-hand gate and the wall on the left. The wagon, No. 34, is ex-WD class 'E'.

Ray Hooley

Nocton Estate. Todds Farm on Nocton Fen. The line, its sleepers hidden by a luxuriant growth of weeds, is obviously well used and typical of the appearance on the fenland. *Redshaw Collection*

Nocton Estate. Wasps Nest, a tiny community at the western edge of the fen. A pair of bogie wagons can be seen to the right of the cottage at the far end with one more in front of the sheds in the middle distance. *Redshaw Collection*

Nocton Estate. Locomotive No. 5 brings a short train of bagged potatoes up the steep climb from Wasps Nest in 1937. The train includes wagon No. 45. The siding in the foreground leads to the nearby sand pit.   *Institute of Agricultural History*

Nocton Estate. Another photograph taken in 1937. This shows a threshing machine at work, powered by the attendant tractor, probably a Fiat. Ten men are working, one taking sacks of grain to the waiting former WD ambulance wagon, No. 73. Because of their propensity to overturn with potatoes the vans were usually used for grain. In addition, the van would keep the grain dry.   *Institute of Agricultural History*

Nocton Estate. The Halls Yard Piggery at Dunston. The older pens remain on the left-hand side with modern ones to the right. Pig muck is being shovelled into one of the four-wheeled wagons. From here it will be taken out for spreading on the fields as fertiliser.   *Redshaw Collection*

Nocton Estate. This photograph was taken in 1950 and shows the Halls Yard Piggery from the opposite direction. By now modernisation of the pens has been completed and a clean track set in concrete serves the central passageway.   *Redshaw Collection*

Nocton Estate. Smith's Potato Crisps introduced a fleet of tractors onto the Estate in 1948. They remained on the farms and their fuel was taken to them by train. For this two bogie wagons were converted to oil tankers and they are seen in these two views, with an unidentified locomotive, filling up from a Bedford tanker.   *Redshaw Collection*

Above: Nocton Estate. The estate yard was, and still is, dominated by the mill. This five-storey concrete building was erected in 1926. The south and east sides are seen here. The railway ran through the building with sidings on the east side and a canopy for vehicles loading or unloading along its eastern face. The estate workshops are to the right.
Redshaw Collection

Left: Nocton Estate. A part-loaded train by the canopy on the east side of the mill.
Redshaw Collection

Nocton Estate. Another view of the east side of the mill with its grass-grown sidings. In front of the four former ambulance vans are three four-wheeled wagons with bogie wagons, including No. 9, nearby. *Redshaw Collection*

Nocton Estate. Shunting in the Estate Yard on 30th March, 1950. The man on the right signals to the driver that the points have been set for the right road. In the background, behind the bogie wagons, are five of the former ambulance vans. *Redshaw Collection*

At its peak, the Estate was using 220 working horses, had 1,000 cattle, which in winter would be in 29 crew yards, up to 3,000 pigs and 2,000 sheep. The railway transported all their food to them, from the mill.

A typical weekly timetable for one engine was: Monday, tractor fuel; Tuesday, water; Wednesday, spare day; Thursday, rations to feedstock; and Friday, water again. In addition, there was seasonal daily traffic in farm produce. When steam-ploughing sets were at work in the fields, a water supply would be provided from a tank wagon stabled at the nearest point.

The service required a large number of vehicles. The wagons were all ex-army. The first rolling stock was 36 small four-wheeled flat ration trucks, ex-WD 'P' class, converted locally to open wagons with the provision of low wooden bodies. They were usually operated in rakes of four, and each one could carry about 1¼ tons. Some were converted to guard's vans, and were provided with letterboxes to extend the local postal services to the isolated farms. They were followed by 53 open bogie wagons, of two types: ex-WD 'D' (Drop Side Open), and 'E' (Well Wagon with Sides), classes. Some had wood, and others steel underframes. Each could carry a five-ton load. There were 12 box bogie wagons, originally ambulance vans, which could carry a six-ton load but tended to overturn when fully loaded, which restricted their use. Last were five 2,000-gallon water tanks for drinking water. In later years, two bogie wagons were converted to carry fuel tanks for the tractor supplies, and two four-wheel wagons were converted to a 'rail bogie' for moving lengths of track around. There were also a number of tip wagons, used in the pig pens and fields for moving water and feed from point to point. These, of about 15 cwt capacity, were always pushed manually. For more details of the rolling stock see Chapter Seven.

A traffic controller noted every wagon movement. All wagons were numbered, the rakes of four-wheel trucks Nos. 1 to 8, the others individually. Painted light grey, they carried their numbers, in white, on one side and one end. At the mill was a large green baize-covered board with an Estate field plan and the railway route marked on it. Each field was numbered, and each wagon number was attached to a pin. The pin was placed in the board to give the location of the wagon. The system was very similar to that used by the Army in the war, and may be attributable to Major Webber.

At the railhead, two copies of a ticket were written out, noting the quantity and type of load, the weight, destination and truck number. One copy was retained, the other attached to the wagon, which the train crew then took to the correct location. For an inward journey, a docket headed N. E. L. R. (Nocton Estate Light Railway) was filled out, noting the wagon number, contents, destination, time required and a train number.

Although not a passenger-carrying enterprise, staff were regularly carried. In the season, gangs of women potato pickers would travel to and from the field in which they were needed, on the return journey often on top of sacks of potatoes. In the mid-1920s an early morning main line train would bring 40 or 50 women to Nocton and Dunston station. They would transfer to open wagons at the railhead using a special platform built for them to the north of the mill.

Nocton Estate. A poor photograph of the interior of the mill, but it does show the loading platform, the siding and the various chutes for delivering feed into railway wagons.

Redshaw Collection

Nocton Estate. The view south of the engine shed and sidings taken from the top of the mill. Some alterations to the track layout to the engine shed had taken place by this time (*see map on page 66*). The siding below the photographer ran through the mill and the dock platform, with its narrow and standard gauge sidings, can be seen on the right.　　　　　*Redshaw Collection*

Nocton Estate. Along and beyond the west side of the mill was the loading dock for the estate's private siding. Here, again under a canopy on the side of the mill, bagged potatoes are transferred from narrow to standard gauge. *Redshaw Collection*

Nocton Estate. The loading dock to the south of the mill with bagged potatoes awaiting transfer. *Redshaw Collection*

Nocton Estate. On the north side of the mill the dock was also used to facilitate transfer to road vehicles. Both of these pictures show bagged potatoes being loaded into lorries to be taken to the Smith's Crisps factory on Newark Road in Lincoln.   *Redshaw Collection*

In 1927, one of the bogies was converted to become the only passenger coach used on the line. The Estate provided for what was believed to be the best shooting estate in the County and the coach was provided specifically for shooting parties. It was known as the *Queen Mary* and had sliding end doors with six windows on each side. There were comfortable individual seats, each with a rack for drinks, and a gun rack for the use of estate shooting parties. It was usually coupled to a box wagon fitted with game racks. There were two rules, the first that the train would leave the Estate yard at precisely 9.00 am on shooting days and that there was to be no firing from the windows.

Other occasions on which passengers used the trains were occasional Sunday School outings in the 1920s from the villages to the River Witham, and once, a coffin and funeral cortège to Nocton Churchyard. Estate workers would be carried from the village out to Wasps Nest, where there was a small social club, and back, for Saturday night Whist Drives. On at least one occasion it was used for a house move. In 1947 an Estate worker moved house from one part of the Fen to another, the family, and their possessions, being moved using two box wagons and two bogie wagons. There were also two Narrow Gauge Railway Society visits, on 15th May, 1955 and 3rd June, 1956. On the first of these members travelled in a train comprising the Nocton coach and one bogie wagon while on the second two open bogie wagons sufficed. On both occasions the engine used was Simplex No. 5.

There were a total of seven Simplex and two Ruston & Hornsby locomotives used on the line together with at least one steam locomotive. The details of these are given in Chapter Six. One Simplex was converted to a snowplough after 1936. The incline up from Wasps Nest was particularly prone to blocking by drifting snow, and the combined power of five engines together was at times needed to clear it. The Simplex engines were fitted with sanders for use in both directions and were capable of hauling loads of 20 to 25 tons on the flat, or a maximum of 12 tons up from Wasps Nest. Locally made timber cabs were provided to protect the driver from the elements. No such luxury was provided for a second seat on the front of the vehicles.

Two steam locomotives were tried out. No information survives about one; the other was a Fowler 0-6-0 tank delivered new to Nocton in 1926. At 11¾ tons it proved too heavy for the track, particularly on the marshy Fenland, and was confined to working west of Wasps Nest. It could haul eight wagons conveying a maximum of 50 tons up the bank. Its weight was its great handicap; on curves it tended to push against the outside rail to the extent that it would leave the track. For this reason it was sold to George Cohen and Sons of Leeds about 1930. It was subsequently recorded as in use at the construction of a reservoir in Upper Weardale, Durham, where it ran in its Nocton livery, and lettered N.E.L.R. At Nocton, a ventilator was put in the roof above the centre road of the engine shed, where it was stabled when not in use.

The Estate's main customer was Smith's Potato Crisps, and they bought the land in 1936. They made no change to the farming methods and continued to use the railway. They introduced mechanisation, starting with a fleet of 24 tractors in 1948, increased to 32 in 1951, but the importance of the railway was still recognised; without it, greater investment in new machinery would be

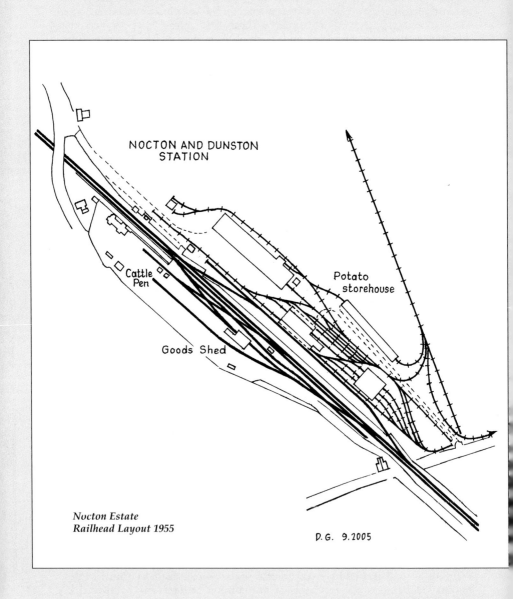

NOCTON AND DUNSTON
STATION

Potato
storehouse

Cattle
Pen

Goods Shed

Nocton Estate
Railhead Layout 1955

D.G. 9.2005

needed. In 1955 it was still transporting 17,000 tons of produce annually, but about this time the decision was taken that, to cut out double handling, farm roads should be improved to give lorries direct field access. By the end of 1960 this had largely been completed and much of the system closed. However, one locomotive, four bogie wagons and some track were retained in use, serving the potato chitting house until July 1969. So closed the last of the county's potato railways. The scrap man moved in, but he did not get it all. A small fruit farm near Edinburgh purchased three lorry loads of track and trucks.

The line had also survived long enough for the growing railway preservation movement to take an interest, and for this reason it is possible to see track, wagons and engines from the Estate today. In 1958 a group of South Humberside narrow gauge railway enthusiasts determined that the area should have its own line. They took advantage of the closure and in 1960 purchased 700 yards of track, one locomotive, No. 5, two bogie vans, two bogie and five four-wheel wagons. These were used to create the Lincolnshire Coast Light Railway at Humberstone, south of Cleethorpes. It was later extended with track from other sources. In 1969, another engine, No. 1, five bogie wagons and one four-wheel wagon followed from Nocton. Subsequently, the Nocton coach also arrived on the site at Humberston, from the scrap yard where it had served as an office for some years. The origin of some of the rolling stock could be seen there, one bogie wagon underframe, supporting an open coach body, still displaying shrapnel damage from 70 years before.

Of particular interest were the bogie vans, built as ambulance vans by the Gloucester Carriage & Wagon Company for the Army in World War I. They are the last survivors of their type and could accommodate nine stretchers together with a bench for those who could sit. Because of their value, a Historic Vehicle Trust was set up to restore these and other surviving wagons. One of the vans and other items of track and rolling stock from Nocton were put on display in the Museum of Army Transport at Beverley but have now moved to the Lincolnshire Coast Light Railway at Winthorpe (*see Chapter Eight*).

Visitors to the Festiniog Railway in Wales can see two surviving bogie wagons acquired by them. The Festiniog took four, Smith's No. 3, which was renumbered 63 in Wales, No. 9, renumbered 62, No. 18, renumbered 60 and No. 35, renumbered 61. Nos. 63 and 61 are in regular use, the latter having since been converted into an oil tank wagon. The other two have been broken up for spares. The well-known narrow gauge equipment manufacturer, Hudson's, built all four.

One former 'P' class ration wagon was acquired by the Amberley Chalk Pits Museum and can be seen there fully restored to its WD state. One of the ambulance vans went to the South Tynedale Railway. It has subsequently been sold on in a dismantled condition and is not currently on display.

And what of Nocton itself? What little remains *in situ* continues to lessen as time grows by. There are remains of the track both inside and outside the mill, and rails are still embedded in a concrete bridge over a drain which was used by coal trains running to the pumping station alongside Nocton Delph. Probably the most interesting feature is one former water tank, not now mounted on a wagon, but sited adjacent to the mill in the Estate yard, serving as a reservoir for emergency firefighting purposes.

Nocton Estate. Immediately north of the dock at the railhead the standard gauge and narrow gauge sidings lay parallel. This was to facilitate loading down from the former to the latter. In the upper photograph empty sacks returned to the Estate are transferred to a lorry, in the 1950s. In the lower photograph a Simplex locomotive, probably No 4, is waiting with the oil train at the lower level.   *(Both) Redshaw Collection*

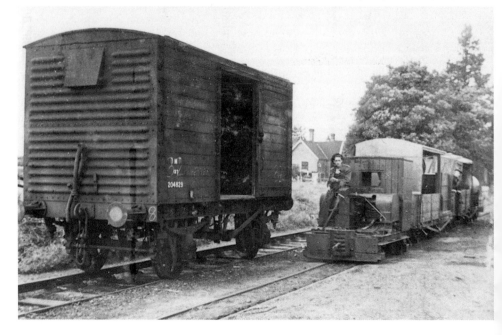

Nocton Estate. Before potatoes could be set in the fields as seed they had to be 'chitted'. The process took place in large glasshouses. This is the one at the railhead, almost 80 metres long, seen from the top of the mill. *Redshaw Collection*

Nocton Estate. In the glasshouse the seed potatoes were laid out in wooden trays and stacked until they begin to sprout green shoots or 'chits'. Only then would they be taken to the fields to be planted. Here, inside the glasshouse in 1950, trays of seed potatoes are being loaded using the light railway running through the centre. *Redshaw Collection*

Nocton Estate. With the seed potatoes safely sown the glasshouse could be turned over to the production of tomatoes. This photograph was taken in 1950.   *Redshaw Collection*

Nocton Estate. The sugar beet factory at Bardney opened in 1927. Sugar beet from the estate was carried to the factory by a grab running on a gantry over the River Witham. Here loaded wagons are being emptied by hand into a hopper from where it is being picked up by the grab.

Author's Collection

Above left: Nocton Estate. In 1927 the railway's only coach was built on a bogie wagon chassis. It was built for shooting parties and here, in the early 1950s, a party stands in front of it. *Redshaw Collection*
Above right: Nocton Estate. A shooting party lunching inside the Nocton coach. In the centre, facing the camera, is Mr J. Ireson, the Estate Manager for many years. *Redshaw Collection*

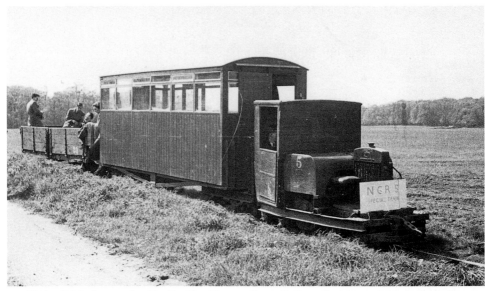

Nocton Estate. Locomotive No. 5 with a Narrow Gauge Railway Society special train, including headboard, on 15th May, 1955. The train is standing somewhere between the railhead and Wasps Nest. One of the sliding end doors of the coach can be seen.   *Ron Redman*

Nocton Estate. Another view of the special train for the visit of the Narrow Gauge Railway Society on 15th May, 1955. This view was taken from the Mill.   *Ron Redman*

Nocton Estate. Physical remains of the railway are now very few. On the loading dock at the mill and set in the concrete of a bridge way down on Nocton Fen are surviving lengths of rail.

(Both) Author

Above: Nocton Estate. A water tank, formerly mounted on an ex-WD bogie wagon, serves a new use holding water for use by the mill in case of fire. *Author*

Right: Nocton Estate. Alongside the route of the line to the south of Nocton cricket field is the former water point. This is the remains of the pipework from which the water tanks would be filled to supply water by rail to the farms down on the fen. It was manufactured by Glenfield & Kennedy of Kilmarnock. *Author*

Finally, the Estate Valuation Books give snapshot information on the extent of the rolling stock and its value. The two Tables which follow are extracts from the Valuation Books of 1947, when the line was around half-way through its life, and for 1964, shortly before closure and when only a small rump of the line was in operation.

Table Four
Nocton Rolling Stock and Valuation, 1947

Item	Value		
	£	s.	d.
No. 1 Loco Engine by Simplex Motor Rail Company	60	18	3
No. 2 Loco Engine - ditto	60	18	3
No. 3 Loco Engine (Diesel)	87	8	8
No. 4 Loco Engine (4 tons)	60	18	3
No. 5 Loco Engine (2½ tons)	60	18	3
1 Petrol Engine Plate Layers Trolley	2	9	0
30 Small Ration Trucks	48	16	6
1 Rail Bogey	3	1	0
3 Guards Vans (scrap)	4	11	5
12 Box Wagons	127	17	8
5 Water Wagons	45	14	4
2 Petrol Tank Trucks (200 gals)	3	0	4
2 Semi Rotary Pumps		14	11
24 Steel Frame Open Trucks	219	19	1
11 Steel Frame Unslung Open Trucks	66	19	5
19 Wood Frame Open Trucks	110	3	0
7 Tip Wagons (scrap)	5	11	7
2 Water Tank Trucks	3	1	0
3 Small Flat Trucks (scrap)	2	5	6
1 Tip Wagon Frame and Wheels		8	9
1 Flat Truck Frame		3	1
20 Large truck Sheets	10	19	2
1 Plate Layers Repair Truck		12	11
14 Lengths various Scrap Rail	1	10	5
3 pairs Wheels and Axles	2	18	0
30 Iron Sleepers	5	17	0
1 Right Angle Crossing		17	6
4 Pairs Switches 22 lbs and 1 Pair 20 lbs	4	11	5
Rail, 726 ft in 16 ft lengths, 284 ft short lengths, 200 ft Length Rail	27	1	0
80 Chains Light Railway (as laid in Main Line)	131	8	6
New Rail Coach	33	0	2
6 Large Railway Sheets (scrap)	7	6	4
4 Small Railway Sheets	4	0	6
8 chain Spare rails and Sleepers (as laid in main line)	15	1	3
No. 6 Loco Engine (Diesel) by Simplex Motor Rail Company	203	16	2
Total	1424	19	5

Source, Estate Valuation Book for 1947, order and descriptions as in the Book.

West Fen Farm, Carrington. The remains of the farm glasshouse, once used for chitting potatoes. The farm railway ran between it and the farm roadway on the right. *Author*

CARRINGTON

West Fen Catchwater Drain

Stickney

West Fen Farm

11

Carrington

Medlam Drain

N

0   ¼   ½
mile

Wragg Hall
Farm

12

Hakerley
Bridge

To Boston

Table Five
Nocton Rolling Stock and Valuation, 1964

Item	Value		
	£	s.	d.
No. 1 Loco Engine by Simplex Rail Co	6	6	7
1 Box Wagon	1	2	0
1 Steel Frame Open truck		18	9
1 Steel Frame Unslung Open Truck		12	8
Total	9	0	0

Source, Estate Valuation Book, 1964. Order and descriptions as in the Book.

11. West Fen Farm, Carrington

This farm was owned by T.J. Ward who also owned Leadenhall Farm at Holbeach St Marks where he laid a light railway about 1914. This makes him an early user but when he laid a line here is not known. It ran southwards from the farm buildings, alongside the Medlam Drain. By the bridge giving access to the farm over the Drain there was a glasshouse. South of here the line turned to the east and ran out into the fields. It was about one mile long.

The sleepers here were concrete and some of them survive. These were 3 ft 6 in. long by 7 in. wide and cast with chamfered top edges. The rails were secured to them with bolts. The gauge was two feet. Potato graves were built in the fields adjacent to the line from where potatoes were bagged for onward transmission. Where the fields were separated from the line by a dyke a plank would be laid over the dyke for the workers to carry sacks of potatoes to the wagons.

It was in use during World War II but not afterwards. It was left *in situ* for some time before being taken up. The sleepers were broken up to form the foundation of new farm roads. Rail was cut up for fence posts and lengths used as clothes posts, as well as runner bean row support, can be found in cottage gardens in the area. The farm glasshouse, without its glass, can still be seen. This is of a well-detailed cast-iron design.

12. Wragg Hall Farm, Carrington

Very little is known about this line. It ran for one mile from the Wragg Hall Farm buildings alongside the B1183 at Carrington, at first east, then south, before reaching Hakerley Bridge, on the road between Carrington and Stickney. It had, therefore, an outlet to a road at both ends. The farm was owned and the light railway operated by T.R. Pick who also farmed land at Deeping St Nicholas. It was horse-worked and is believed to have been 2 ft gauge. The dates it was laid and taken up are not known but it was still in operation during World War II.

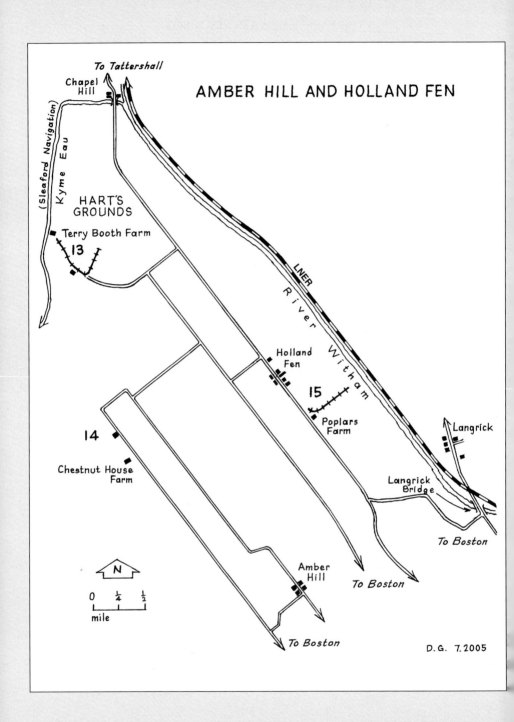

AMBER HILL AND HOLLAND FEN

To Tattershall

Chapel Hill

(Sleaford Navigation)
Kyme Eau

HART'S GROUNDS

Terry Booth Farm

13

LNER

River Witham

Holland Fen

15

Poplars Farm

Langrick

14

Chestnut House Farm

Langrick Bridge

To Boston

Amber Hill

To Boston

To Boston

N

0   ¼   ½
mile

To Boston

D.G. 7.2005

13. Terry Booth Farm, Hart's Grounds

The date that rails were laid on this farm is not known but thought to be in the late 1920s or early 1930s. The land was farmed by J. Measures. He had family ties with a Mr Atkinson who farmed at Victoria Farm, Deeping High Bank near Spalding. A line was in operation here (*see Victoria Farm, Deeping St Nicholas below*) and it may be because of this that the line at Terry Booth Farm was laid. It took the form of an L-shape, ½ mile-long, with its two extremes within the fields. It was laid by the farm labour using 18 ft lengths of rail with wooden sleepers.

At the half-way point, alongside a farm road, was a farmhouse and a range of farm buildings. The buildings included a glasshouse used for potato chitting as well as a transhipment shed. This shed survived up to 2001. It was about 20 x 30 feet, of corrugated iron. Inside the rails ran up onto a loading dock from which potatoes were loaded onto lorries. The dock could hold three wagons.

At harvesting potato graves were built along the edge of the fields alongside the track. After they were riddled and bagged sacks of potatoes were carried to the transhipment shed. Horses hauled the wagons although latterly a Case three-wheeled tractor was used. The line was used up to the mid-1950s. The rails remained *in situ* until 1968 when they were cut up for fence posts. Some of these posts still survive along field boundaries and can be seen alongside the nearby Kyme Eau. This forms part of the Sleaford Navigation and the fence is alongside the towpath here. The sleepers were burnt, many of them as fuel by itinerant Irish labourers who were employed as seasonal workers.

14. Chestnut House Farm, Amber Hill

This farm was owned by the Pocklington family who also laid a railway on their farm at Poplars Farm, Holland Fen. Nothing more has been discovered about the line laid here.

15. Poplars Farm, Holland Fen

This was one of the farms in the area farmed by the Pocklington family. Poplars Farm lies between North Forty Foot Bank - the road running alongside the North Forty Foot Drain - and the River Witham. The line was about ⅗ mile long, running from the potato growing land near to the river to the farm buildings adjacent to the road. It ran diagonally across the grass paddock next to the farm buildings to finish parallel to the road where there was a loading dock and glasshouse.

The dates of its operation are not known although there are local memories of playing on it in 1937.

Some rails, now cut up for fence posts, survive around the farm. These are in 12 ft lengths, cut to use for fencing pheasant rearing and release pens. The pen fencing had to be high to keep foxes out. Other rails support a gravestone,

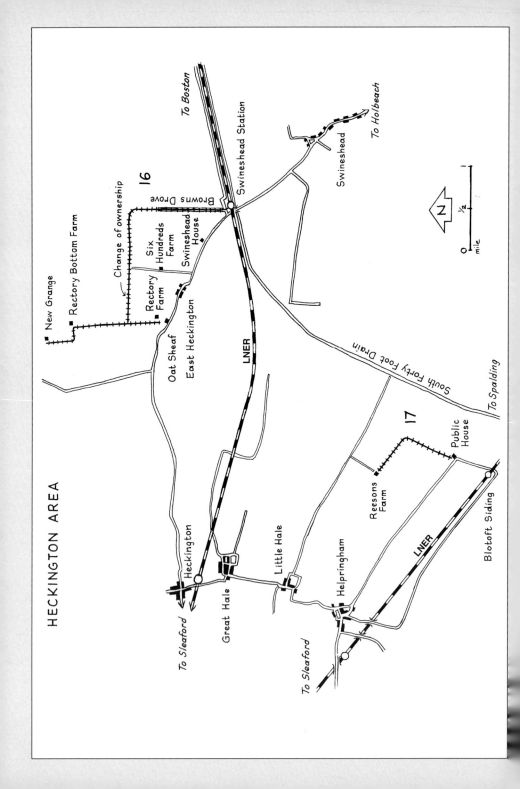

HECKINGTON AREA

New Grange

Rectory Bottom Farm

Change of ownership

16

Six Hundreds Farm

Rectory Farm

Swineshead House

Oat Sheaf

East Heckington

Browns Drove

To Boston

Swineshead Station

Swineshead

To Holbeach

N

0 ½ mile

LNER

Heckington

To Sleaford

Great Hale

Little Hale

Helpringham

To Sleaford

Reesons Farm

17

Public House

South Forty Foot Drain

To Spalding

LNER

Blotoft Siding

perhaps the most unusual use for narrow gauge rail today in the County. This marks the grave of Elizabeth Wells who died in 1838 and was buried in her garden, as was her husband. The house and buildings of the farm here are long gone. The burial plot was left fenced off. The gravestone was broken by cattle that broke through the fence but was remounted on the stub and is now held in place by pairs of narrow gauge rails.

16. Rectory Farm and Six Hundreds Farm, East Heckington

E. and F. Bowser were cousins who had adjacent farms on Heckington Fen. In the early 1920s E. Bowser laid 1¾ miles of rail on his Rectory Farm and F. Bowser 2¼ miles on his Six Hundreds Farm. That on Rectory Farm linked the Fenland fields with the main farmyard adjacent to what is now the A17 road, behind a pub, the Oat Sheaf, where there was a transhipment dock for road vehicles. The other ran direct into Swineshead station yard, on the line between Sleaford and Boston, where there was a timber dock for loading direct to and from railway wagons. The lines were also linked to give E. Bowser an outlet over his neighbour's line to the station.

Although the lines were connected each opted for a different method of tracklaying. The rails on Rectory farm were dog-spiked to wooden sleepers. On the other farm, the rails were fixed to metal sleepers. The latter proved to be less effective, deteriorating more quickly than timber and causing a continual maintenance problem, although quicker to lay initially. All the work on both farms was carried out by farm labour.

For most of the route the line ran across farmland, but on the approach to Swineshead station the line ran alongside the road known as Browns Drove. Before passing into the station yard there was a level crossing over the Sleaford to Boston road. This had no gates and was protected by standard road sign proclaiming 'crossing - no gates', with the black silhouette of a steam railway engine.

The main traffic was potatoes, beet pulp, corn and cattle cake. The lines were both worked by horses. There were a number, possibly up to 15, of trucks, at least six owned by E. Bowser. Each carried a maximum of 33 cwt, a full load for one horse being five tons on three wagons.

Farm roads replaced both railways in 1945. No traces remain.

17. Reesons Farm, Little Hale

The date of construction of 1¼ miles of line on this farm is not known. However, the farm was purchased by the Reeson brothers about 1931 and it may have been in existence prior to that. It was worked by horses, the gauge unknown.

From the 'main' line sidings were laid to a number of fields. There were three small trucks. The line ran to a small dock at the rear of a small, isolated house, at the end of North Fen Road on Helpringham Fen. From here a road ran ½ mile

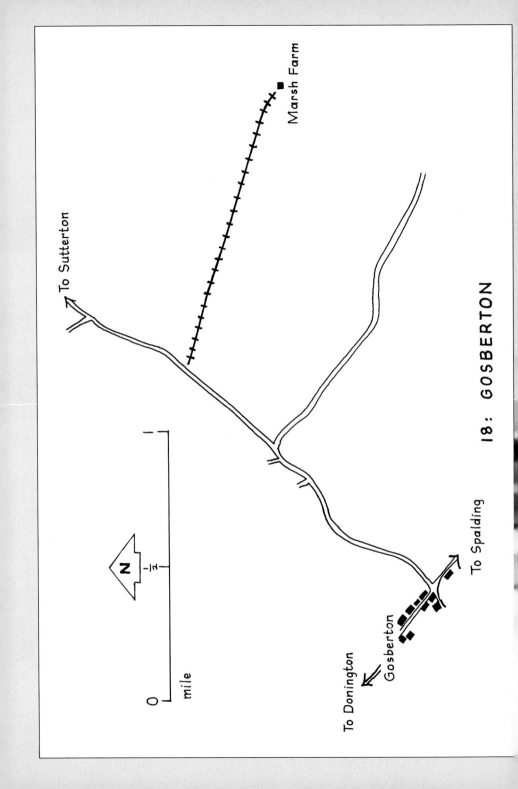

To Sutterton

Marsh Farm

N

mile

0 ½

To Donington

Gosberton

To Spalding

18: GOSBERTON

south to Blotoft Siding on the former Great Northern & Great Eastern Joint Railway, between Sleaford and Spalding.

Three miles south-east of Helpringham station, Blotoft was one of a number of sidings provided on this line, between stations, primarily to tap agricultural traffic. Potatoes, grain and sugar beet, the latter bound for the Spalding Sugar Beet Factory, were the main crops carried on the farm railway.

The buildings behind which the loading dock was sited have long been demolished. The line was removed in about 1941 as the equipment had become unreliable and the track needed re-laying. Lengths of rail were cut up and reused as fence posts around the farm. The concrete dock still survives at the point where the railway ended.

18. Marsh Farm, Gosberton

A line was laid here, alongside a silt road, for 1$\frac{1}{10}$ miles between Marsh Farm and the main road between Gosberton and Sutterton. Horse-worked, and with a loading dock by the main road, it was laid by the owner of Marsh Farm, W.D. Cook, a potato merchant from Kirton. Following his death the land was farmed by an uncle for a short time before being taken over by the Lindsey County Council and divided into a number of smallholdings. This date this happened is not known but it is believed to have been before 1939. The railway was probably removed at that time when it was replaced by a concrete road serving the smallholdings. The lane serving these today is now called Cooks Road.

19. Manor Farm, Frampton

Built in 1912 or 1913, this line was on land owned by W. Dennis & Sons, and operated by them; 1$\frac{1}{5}$ miles long, including one short branch off the 'main' line, it was 2 ft gauge and worked by horse, until its closure in about 1941.

20. Lammings Marsh Farm, Fosdyke

Another farm forming part of the Dennis Estates, also known as Ireland's Farm, this line has a similar history to that of its nearby neighbour, Manor Farm at Frampton. Laid immediately before World War I, it succumbed in World War II, in about 1941. It was $\frac{1}{5}$ mile long, running eastwards on to land reclaimed from the saltmarsh, was 2 ft gauge and horse-worked.

Dennis's adoption of a standard 2 ft gauge for all their estate railways in the county, here, as at Nocton and at Deeping St Nicholas, meant that rolling stock was interchangeable, and transfers would take place from time to time reflecting demand at individual locations or, indeed, eventual contraction as lines began to close.

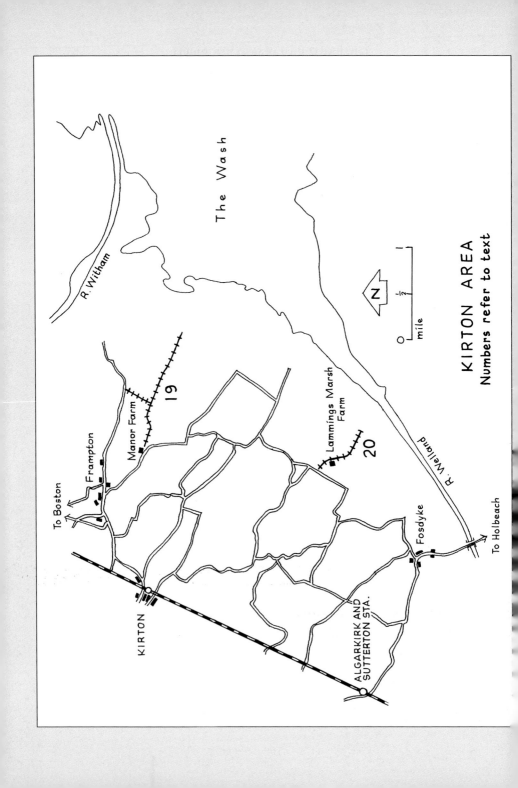

The Wash

R. Witham

To Boston

Frampton

Manor Farm

19

Lammings Marsh Farm

20

R. Welland

Fosdyke

To Holbeach

KIRTON

ALGARKIRK AND SUTTERTON STA.

KIRTON AREA
Numbers refer to text

N

mile $\frac{1}{2}$

21. Leadenhall Farm, Holbeach St Marks

Known as Leadenhall today, in the 1930s it was Leaden Hall. The 3⅓ miles of line on this farm were largely built by his own farm labour by T.J. Ward, around 1914. The 'main' line ran north-eastwards from the farmstead for two miles to terminate adjacent to the sea bank in fields appropriately called the 'newlands', being at that time the most recently reclaimed from the saltmarsh on the edge of the Wash. There were three short branches, one from the eastern terminus, south towards Lapwater Farm, and one each to two groups of buildings on the sea bank, Barn Farm and Hospital Cottages.

The line employed a number of trucks, of which up to six at a time would be hauled by the farm's horses; the gauge is unrecorded. In the spring, seed potatoes and fertiliser would be carried out into the fields for planting. Potatoes were harvested in October and put into clamps. From these clamps the produce would be riddled to grade them for size, and removed for sale as required. Cereal crops were also grown but as these were harvested in the late summer when carts did not get bogged down, then taken to the farmyard for threshing, less use was made of the railway.

Trucks were linked to the horse with a chain. Once started, he knew his job and his master had only to open and close farmgates as he passed. The animal walked on a path alongside the rails, only walking on the track if he needed purchase on the sleepers. In the farmyard at Leadenhall was a large shed adjacent to the road, with doors at either end, into which the railway ran. As they neared the shed the horse would be slowed; two-thirds of the way into the shed the chain was slipped, and the horse, without stopping, walked out of the other end. The trucks came to a halt against a stop at the end of the track and a sack would be thrown under the wheels as a scotch to stop them running back. Here they were unloaded into carts or lorries. In addition to the shed two sidings ran, one either side, into two greenhouses.

On this farm it was not unusual for workers to rig a temporary mast and sail to a truck to travel to or from the fields. However, they had to be adept at judging speed when approaching one bend, and slow down by dropping the sail. On occasions when the bend was taken too fast, the truck left the rails and threw its passengers into a dyke. Rerailing was no problem as one man could do this with an empty truck quite easily.

The line is believed to have closed just after the end of World War II, and was dismantled. Until January 1986 the transhipment shed stood alongside the road at Leadenhall Farm, but was then demolished. No trace of the line remains. Alongside the road there is a greenhouse. Although not the same as when the line was in operation it stands on the site of one which was there then.

22. Wraggmarsh House Farm, Weston

Credit goes to George Caudwell for being the first man to use a light railway on his land, and it was most probably part of the Wraggmarsh House Farm on which these rails were laid (*see Chapter Four*). It is no surprise that Mr Caudwell

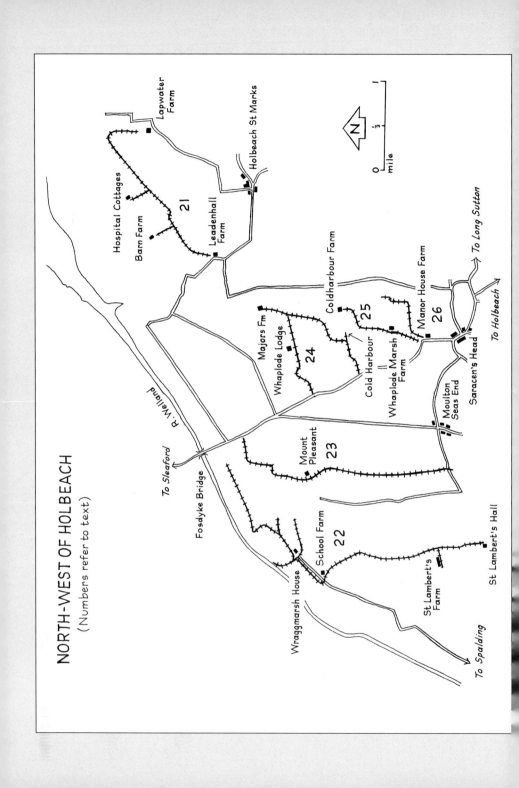

NORTH-WEST OF HOLBEACH
(Numbers refer to text)

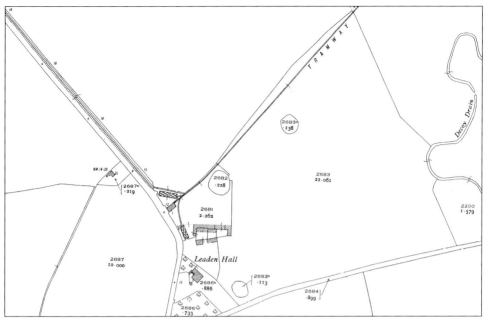

Leadenhall Farm. The end of the line, in the farmyard. The three sidings ran into the shed, in the centre alongside the road, and into two glasshouses, one on either side.

Reproduced from the 25", 1931 Edition, Ordnance Survey Map

Leadenhall Farm. The transhipment shed adjacent to the road in January 1986, a week before it was demolished. The rails entered at the far end and the horse would walk out of the white doors as its hauling chain was slipped.   *Author*

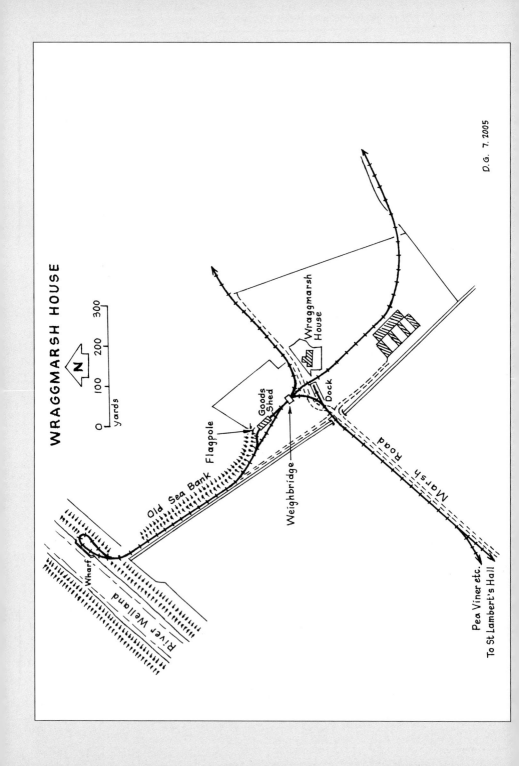

WRAGGMARSH HOUSE

N

0 100 200 300
yards

River Welland

Wharf

Old Sea Bank

Flagpole

Goods
Shed

Weighbridge

Wraggmarsh
House

Dock

Marsh Road

Pea Viner etc.
To St Lambert's Hall

D.G. 7. 2005

Wraggmarsh House. Horse power on the farm. A very rare photograph of the most common motive power used on farm railways. This one is hauling peas on their way to be vined.

George Hay

Wraggmarsh House. The Hudson locomotive, supplied to the farm in the early 1930s, with a load of peas. Hudson's were well known manufacturers of narrow gauge railway equipment, making their name originally with the supply of military light railway material in the latter half of World War I.   *E. Sismey*

Wraggmarsh House. Pea vining in progress in the 1930s. The traction engine is at work driving the machinery that is separating the pea pods from the pea vine. Of railway interest are the two wagons on the line on the right of the picture. One of these, plank-sided, carries coal and the other, an upright skip, water for the engine.   *E. Sismey*

Wraggmarsh House. Caudwell's wharf, on the River Welland, in 1914. The horse on the left is supplying the power to work the crane. This is being used to unload a barge. Timber, and full sacks are being loaded onto a rake of flat wagons while a second rake waits its turn further round the loop.   *E. Sismey*

was in the van as far as railways were concerned, for he was a great innovator. He designed, and had built, a variety of items of agricultural equipment, not always a success, and was one of the first farmers in the country to use an aircraft for crop spraying.

Mr Caudwell purchased Wraggmarsh Farm in 1908, and extended his holding in the following years by adding land eastwards to Fosdyke and south to St Lambert's Hall, which then became his home. One of the advantages of the farm was that it lay alongside the River Welland down which passed barges bringing in, and taking away, agricultural goods and produce. The haulage distance from existing river wharves was a problem and so, before 1909, Mr Caudwell built his own, on the river near to Wraggmarsh House. He erected a derrick, worked by a horse, and purchased two small wooden barges for his own use.

Also before 1909, he started building his light railway, and by 1915 he had about 4 miles of line, from the wharf to Wraggmarsh House, thence into the fields, and down to St Lambert's Farm. Although probably the first mile of this was built by a German contractor, the rest was laid by the farm's own labour. The line was worked by horses, it was of 2 ft gauge, and was equipped with about 40 small, flat four-wheel trucks, and 12 steel, truck-mounted tanks for water. A horse would haul three trucks loaded with up to six tons.

The year 1915 was a notable one for the farm. The wharf had soon proved inadequate for the traffic so a new one was built, with a steam crane to replace the wooden derrick. A small steam tug, *Leo*, and three large barges came to replace the original boats. Loads of up to 80 tons at a time travelled between the wharf and Boston and Kings Lynn, taking out corn, peas and potatoes for sale and bringing in fertilizer, seeds and seed potatoes, as well as coal for domestic purposes and use by steam traction engines. The rails were extended almost to Fosdyke, and to St Lambert's Hall, reaching their total extent of six miles. Chitting houses for seed potatoes were built at St Lambert's Farm, and a range of buildings, including a pea viner, were built alongside Marsh Road, the latter served by several sidings reached by both points and turntables.

Between Wraggmarsh House and the wharf a goods shed containing a siding was erected. Any arriving materials not immediately required in the fields were brought here, fertiliser for example. An interesting method of working was adopted. Empty wagons would be taken to the wharf by horse, but as the wharf was on top of the riverbank, they returned by gravity. The wharf and shed were not in sight of one another because an old sea bank intervened. On top of this bank, by the goods shed, a flagpole was erected. When the men were ready for another load the flag was hauled down and trucks would be pushed off the wharf to run on their own. The short sharp gradient off the bank soon ended, giving way to level track, and by the time the vehicles reached the shed they had almost stopped.

In the 1920s two lorries were purchased for local haulage. To enable them to be loaded a dock was built at Wraggmarsh; a siding was laid on this from which produce could be transhipped to be taken, by road, to Spalding.

By 1930, time and heavy traffic were taking their toll on the track and it was decided to replace much of it, and re-equip the line with new rolling stock,

Wraggmarsh House. The wharf on the River Welland with the steam tug, *Leo,* alongside. This is the later wharf, built in 1915, including a steam crane. The depth of water at low tide is clearly demonstrated by the two bathing belles.   *E. Sismey*

Wraggmarsh House. In the 1930s Caudwell's tug *Leo* sank in the river, by the wharf. In this view its funnel pokes forlornly above the water marking its temporary resting place. Despite his best efforts Mr Caudwell could not raise it and a firm from Hull were called in to do the job. It went on to give further years of good service. On the wharf the steam crane and its boiler can be seen.   *E. Sismey*

Wraggmarsh House. In the early 1930s the coaster *Castlerock* was a frequent visitor to the wharf. Its usual cargo would be fertiliser from the London Docks or seed potatoes from Scotland. Farmworkers would earn extra money unloading its cargo.   *E. Sismey*

Wraggmarsh House. One of the uses of the line was to carry coal for domestic use from the wharf to the houses on the farm. In the early days of the line a flat wagon is being unloaded. This is a good illustration of the type of wagon in use as well as the clothes worn by farmworkers at the time. *E. Sismey*

Wraggmarsh House. The farm loading dock still survives and is seen here in 1986. A siding ran up onto it from the right. The line from the wharf ran left and right immediately beyond the far end and branches from this ran both to and from the camera along the roadway. *Author*

including a locomotive. In 1930 work began on relaying between Wraggmarsh Farm and St Lambert's Farm with heavier track on concrete sleepers. A local builder made the sleepers on the farm, and the new track was laid by Irish labour taken on for the job. The work was soon completed and, in 1931, 120 new trucks and 20 larger tank wagons together with a locomotive powered by a Ford tractor engine were supplied by Messrs Hudson's of Leeds. The locomotive was a model described by the manufacturer as their 'Go-Go Tractor'. The records of the Industrial Railway Society record that two of these locomotives were supplied new to George Caudwell in 1932 but oral history has only recalled one. If a second was supplied it may have worked at one of the other Caudwell farms in the County. The new trucks were larger than the old, being six feet square. Supplied flat, they were later fitted with removable sides, the sides being fitted for carrying sugar beet or coal. The trucks that were replaced were taken to the Red House Farm railway, at Dawsmere, also owned by the Caudwell family. From now on, the engine was used for traffic between the two farms, horses still being used on the branches.

Much of the track that was replaced remained on the farms, and was made up into lengths of prefabricated track with metal sleepers. At various places around the system, points were installed from where track could be temporarily laid across the fields to wherever needed. These temporary lines were worked by horses, which brought the loaded trucks to the main line for collection by the locomotive.

In the 1930s the farm roads were improved. A barge would be sent to Snettisham, in Norfolk, and beached at low tide. It was then loaded with gravel, floated off on the high tide, and brought back to the wharf, unloaded into trucks and taken by rail to where it was needed.

Closure of the railway came after the war, in 1947, when the engine and rolling stock were sold. The rails remained to be taken up for reuse, as necessary, mainly as fence posts. Today, almost the only remnant is the loading dock.

23. *Moulton Marsh Light Railway*

Known to have been in existence before 1914, this was a three mile route from Moulton Seas End in the south, to a point adjacent to what is now the A17 main road, half a mile south of Fosdyke Bridge. There were loading docks at either end. Its gauge is not recorded; it was always horse-worked.

The land was in the ownership of Lord Boston when the line was built, and was purchased by W. Dennis & Sons who operated the line until sold again in 1955. Much of the line went out of use in 1946, but the presence of the line is mentioned in the sale particulars for the farm at the northern end of the line in 1955. About one mile remained at that time.

At one time Dennis's proposed to extend the line northwards crossing the main road, then running parallel to it to the wharf at Fosdyke Bridge, but this was not done. It was built entirely on private land, except for a road level crossing at its southern end, where farmbuildings were sited on both sides. Here was one of the line's two sidings, the other being at Mount Pleasant, the farm at about the mid-point of the line.

Moulton Marsh Light Railway. The site of the southern terminus in 1986. The line ran along the route of the farm road and ended here as two sidings. In 1929 there were no buildings here at all.   *Author*

Moulton Marsh Light Railway. A loading dock adjacent to the present day A17 south of Fosdyke Bridge. The railway terminated here after following the line of the cart track.   *Author*

24. Majors Farm, Whaplode Marsh

Known as Wards Farm in 1929, a total of about three miles of track was laid on this farm in the early 20th century. Its gauge is not known. It ran south from Majors Farm to Cold Harbour, with two branches westwards to the present-day A17 road. Both of these had a loading dock adjacent to the road. There were no sidings.

For most of its life horses provided the motive power, but a petrol locomotive was also used. It was built in the farm workshops and was a conversion of a truck and an old Morris car, using only the engine, gearbox and transmission. A second gearbox was fitted to enable it to travel at the same speed in either direction. It was in use from 1937 to 1943, and was faster than a horse. It was capable of hauling a six-ton load.

Much of the line was taken out of use in 1946, but the short branch from Cold Harbour to the main road lingered on until the early 1950s.

25. Whaplode Marsh Farm, Saracen's Head, Whaplode

Running for 1¼ miles from Cold Harbour Farm, south via Whaplode Marsh Farm to the main road near to the Manor House at Saracen's Head, this line was owned and operated by Birch and Bulmer. The gauge is not known, and it was horse-worked. The date of construction and closure is not known, although it was being used in the late 1920s, and it did survive until at least 1946. It had disappeared, however, by 1950.

At its southern terminus stands the only surviving relic of the line. Adjacent to what is now a bypassed section of the A17 stands a large black corrugated-iron and timber shed. This was used to tranship farm produce from railway trucks into road wagons and lorries. The OS map, surveyed in 1929 and published in 1931, shows that the line had one siding and that ran into this shed.

26. Manor House, Saracen's Head, Whaplode

This may well have been the last farm railway built in the County. It does not appear on the 1931 Ordnance Survey Map, as did its neighbour at Whaplode Marsh Farm, so it may have been constructed after that time. The Manor House Farm was then farmed by the Crawley family, who most probably built the line.

It ran from The Manor for a mile out into the fields, its distinctive mapped shape indicating that it ran around their edges. It was in use until the early 1950s, which makes it one of the latest survivors in this area. The gauge is not known.

27. Lundy's Farm, Holbeach St Marks

This was one of George Caudwell's farms, on which, in 1913, following the success of his Wraggmarsh House railway, he laid almost three miles of 2 ft gauge track. It ran from a point accessible by road, east and north out on to the marsh. It was horse-worked. In 1914, at the terminus by the road a wooden transhipment shed was built which stood until demolished in the 1990s. The line was removed in about 1950.

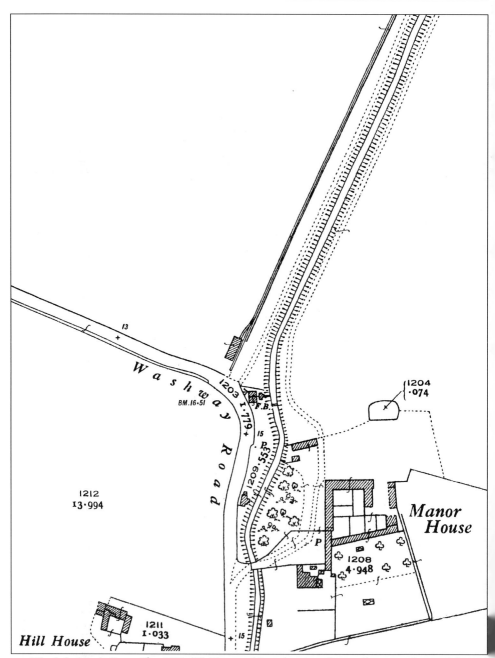

Whaplode Marsh Farm. The 1929 OS Map revision showing the southern terminus of the Whaplode Marsh Farm Railway. The line ended adjacent to Washway Road with one siding running into the goods shed.   *Reproduced from the 25", 1931 Edition, Ordnance Survey Map*

Whaplode Marsh Farm. An isolated shed standing at the edge of a vast Fenland field. This was the southern terminus of a line which followed the route of the road to, and beyond, the farm in the background. The line terminated between the shed and the road with one siding running into the shed from the far end.   *Author*

Lundy's Farm. The goods transhipment shed near to the road leading down to the farmyard. Of timber construction it was built for the line in 1914.   *Author*

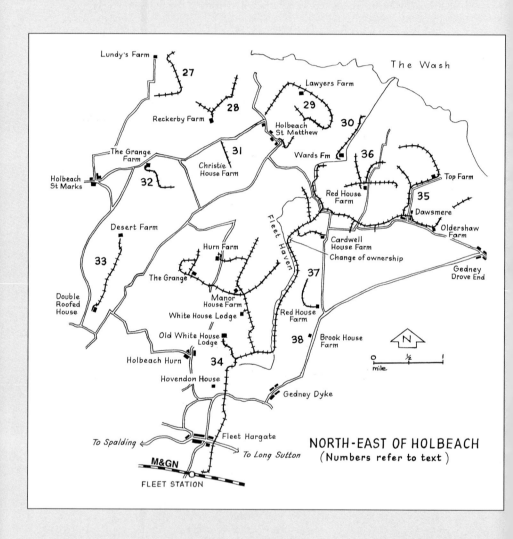

Lundy's Farm

27

28

Reckerby Farm

The Grange
Farm

Holbeach
St Marks

32

31

Christie
House Farm

Desert Farm

33

Double
Roofed
House

The Grange

Hurn Farm

Manor
House Farm

White House Lodge

Old White House
Lodge

Holbeach Hurn

34

Hovendon House

To Spalding

M&GN

FLEET STATION

Fleet Hargate

To Long Sutton

Gedney Dyke

Lawyers Farm

29

Holbeach
St Matthew

Wards Fm

30

36

Red House
Farm

Top Farm

35

Dawsmere

Oldershaw
Farm

Cardwell
House Farm

Change of ownership

Gedney
Drove End

37

Red House
Farm

38

Brook House
Farm

The Wash

N

0   ½   1
mile

NORTH-EAST OF HOLBEACH
(Numbers refer to text)

Fleet Haven

28. Reckerby Farm, Holbeach St Matthew

George Thompson Farms Ltd used a one mile, horse-worked light railway on their Reckerby Farm. The gauge is not known, neither is the date on which it was built. Running generally north-eastwards from the farmyard, following the route of, for much of the way, an old sea bank, to the present sea bank. There was also a branch from the farmyard to the north- west. It was dismantled in 1940.

29. Lawyers Farm, Holbeach St Matthew

This land was farmed by William Caudwell & Son who, in 1923, built a railway from a loading dock at Acre House Farm in Holbeach St Matthew northwards to the sea bank. In 1926 this was extended westwards to Lawyers Farm and then south to another loading dock at the other end of Holbeach St Matthew. Essentially a loop, it linked all the fields, including land re-claimed from the sea, with the farm buildings, and, at either end, the road to the east and west of the village. It was horse-worked, is believed to have been 2 ft gauge, and was built by the farm's own workers to carry potatoes, in sacks, to the loading docks for transfer to road transport. Approximately 25 to 30 flat wagons were used, each carried one ton in weight. They were supplied by a German company, Koppel & Heinstem, specialists in the manufacture of narrow gauge railway equipment. Whether this firm supplied the original equipment for the first potato railway is not known, but it is believed that they equipped several Holbeach area farms. Here, the wagons were used in sets of three, one set being drawn by one horse.

Closed in the early 1940s, when the farm changed from arable to cattle and sheep, the rails were put to a new use. The livestock created a demand for fencing, and this was made from redundant track. The wooden bodies of the trucks were scrapped as they had begun to rot, but the underframes were sold to a customer in the South of England. The two loading docks are the only surviving features of this line.

30. Wards Farm, Holbeach St Matthew

J.J. Bemrose & Son built one mile of line from their fields to Wards Farm around 1920. It was horse-worked, and closed about 1940. No other details are known.

31. Christie House Farm, Holbeach St Matthew

This line, at ⅗ mile, has the distinction of being the shortest in the County. It was built by A. H. Worth of Christie House Farm, and of 2 ft gauge. Horse-worked, it ran from a loading dock by the road straight into the fields. It served no farmyard, and was one of those lines on which children would ride a wagon as it was pushed off the dock.

Lawyers Farm. These two views show the surviving loading docks at either end of the line. The one in the top photograph is that east of Holbeach St Matthew, alongside the road. The picture below shows the other which lies alongside a farm track, off the road from Holbeach St Matthew to the seashore. *(Both) Author*

Used mainly for potatoes, between June and September each year, there were a number of flat wagons. Each would carry about one ton of potatoes, and a horse could pull up to four, fully loaded.

Built around 1920, it was replaced by a road during World War II.

32. The Grange Farm, Holbeach St Marks

This line was built at some time before 1920 by H.P. Carter who owned the farm until that time. After 1920 it was acquired by R.P. Worth & Co. The gauge is believed to be 2 ft and very light 9 lb. per yard rail was used. It ran from the farm buildings out for almost three-quarters of a mile into the fields. In the farmyard it ran into and through a small tumbledown shed.

The line had three small flat trucks, one of which sported a large horizontal brake wheel, which were horse-hauled. It went out of use during World War II.

There are several lengths of rail still on this farm cut up and used mainly as fence posts, but also a number of complete lengths tucked away in the rafters of various buildings.

In common with some other similar farms, several local people have fond memories of their childhood when they used to play with the system, giving one another rides.

33. Desert Farm, Holbeach Marsh

Little is known of this two mile line. The date of construction is not certain, but it was in existence in the late 1920s. Frank Dring, of Double Roofed House, farmed the land at that time at its southern extremity, so it was probably he who built it.

It was of 2 ft gauge and probably only horse-worked. It ran to a loading dock at its southern end and within the Double Roofed House farmyard. Near to the

The Grange, Holbeach St Marks. In 1986, rails lie once again in the farmyard in the approximate position they last lay forty years before. Weighing only 9 lb. per yard, they were easily lifted out of a farm shed in whose rafters they were stored.   *Author*

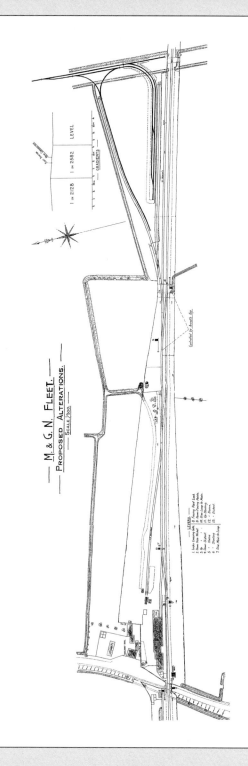

— M. & G. N. FLEET. —
— PROPOSED ALTERATIONS. —
SCALE 1/500.

GRADIENTS

1 in 2 1/28	1 in 2582	LEVEL

LEVERS
1. Goods Crossing Gate.
2. Down Side Wicket.
3. Up "
4. Down Distant.
5. " Home.
6. " Starter.
7. Dim Main to Loop.
8. Facing Pant Lock.
9. Down Facing Pants.
10. Down Loop to Main.
11. Up Starting.
12. " Home.
13. " Distant.

Controlled by Frisby Key.

Fleet Light Railway. Fleet station and the proposed alterations to the layout to serve the terminus of the Fleet Light Railway. The plan was prepared by the Midland & Great Northern Joint Railway Traffic Manager's Office in 1909 prior to the opening of the Light Railway. The siding alongside the M&GN is alongside the loading dock. The one to the north has a narrow gauge siding alongside at ground level.

northern edge of the latter the lines only siding ran into a small shed. It seems to have survived World War II and to have been still in use in 1946, as it appears on maps of that time. By 1951, although the track remained, it was out of use. No trace of it can be found today.

34. Fleet Light Railway

Variously quoted as having been 1 ft 11⅝ in., 1 ft 11¾ in., and 2 ft gauge, the Fleet Light Railway was built in 1909 by A.H. Worth. It served the family farms north of Fleet Hargate, and linked them with Fleet station between Spalding and Kings Lynn on what was then part of the Midland & Great Northern Joint Railway. All the track and equipment was purchased new for the line, nothing was second-hand.

By the early 1930s it was 13 miles in extent, serving White House Lodge, Manor House Farm, The Grange and Hurn Farm, as well as reaching into many of the fields. Built on private land, it crossed public roads at four places. There was also, from about 1921, an end-on junction with the system in the Dawsmere area owned by J.H. Thompson Farms Ltd, and locomotive-hauled trains of the latter worked over Worth's track to reach Fleet station.

Fleet station was nine miles east of Spalding. Never a busy passenger station, there was a loop for the use of goods trains only on this section of single line, and two sidings catered for the local goods traffic. Worth's proposal to site their terminus to the east of the station was welcomed by the M&GN, who provided standard gauge sidings into the Light Railway terminus. The plan prepared in 1909 by the Midland & Great Northern Railway shows two sidings, one ran along the south side of a dock, six feet high, on top of which ran the Light Railway. The other was alongside a narrow gauge siding, both at ground level. The 1929 Ordnance Survey map, by comparison, shows three standard gauge sidings, with an additional one alongside the north side of the dock.

The only alteration to the main line was the moving of the points giving access to the loop at its eastern end, to enable engines to run-round wagons which had to be taken out of the existing yard and put into the new sidings. Access to the new sidings was by tablet instruments controlled by Annett's Key. The loop was also used by goods trains to enable passenger trains to pass without delay. The M&GN notified the Board of Trade of the proposed siding alterations here, by letter and plan as they were required by law to do, on 23rd October, 1909. In that submission they stated that they were 'about to commence' the work.

North of the dock, by the Light Railway, a weighbridge was constructed by Worths.

For the opening of the line, about 16 flat four-wheel trucks were supplied, and horses provided the motive power. Because of the increasing length of track, and the greater weight of produce carried, two small petrol-engined locomotives were provided in 1923 and 1924. These soon proved inadequate for the task, and were replaced in 1925 by a 20 hp locomotive fitted with a Dorman 2JO petrol engine, delivered new to Fleet on 17th August, 1925. This was Motor Rail, Simplex, Works No. 3759. It weighed 2½ tons, its gauge recorded as 600 mm. A second locomotive with a diesel engine, sanding gear and a small cab, was delivered new to Fleet on 18th October, 1933. This was another Simplex,

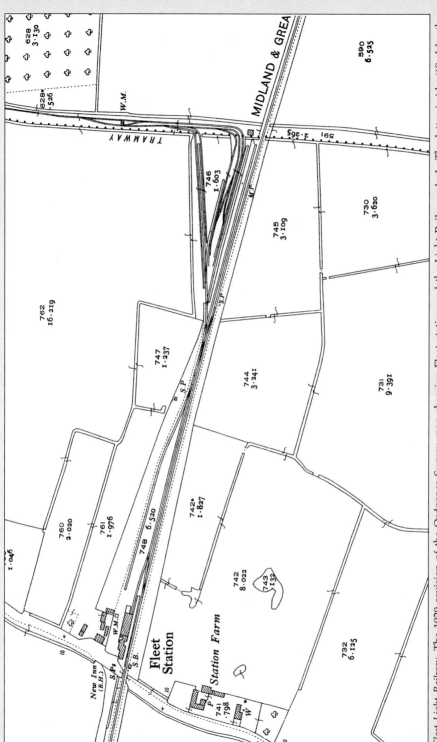

Fleet Light Railway. The 1929 revision of the Ordnance Survey map showing Fleet station and the Light Railway dock. The latter is identified by the description 'TRAMWAY'. The weighbridge hut is identified as W.M. The differences between the original M&GN proposal plan and this survey are an additional standard gauge siding along the north side of the dock together with additional narrow gauge sidings.

Reproduced from the 25″, 1931 Edition, Ordnance Survey Map

Fleet Light Railway. A loaded train on the fen. The unidentified locomotive has a home made cab to protect the driver from the biting wind and rain. The wagons carry bagged potatoes. The tarpaulin alongside the locomotive has probably been erected as a windbreak behind which potatoes are being removed from a grave for sorting and bagging. *A.H. Worth & Co.*

Fleet Light Railway. A shooting party about to depart for a day's sport. Canine and human passengers were carried on flat bogie wagons. These wagons were supplied to the line in 1925. *A.H. Worth & Co.*

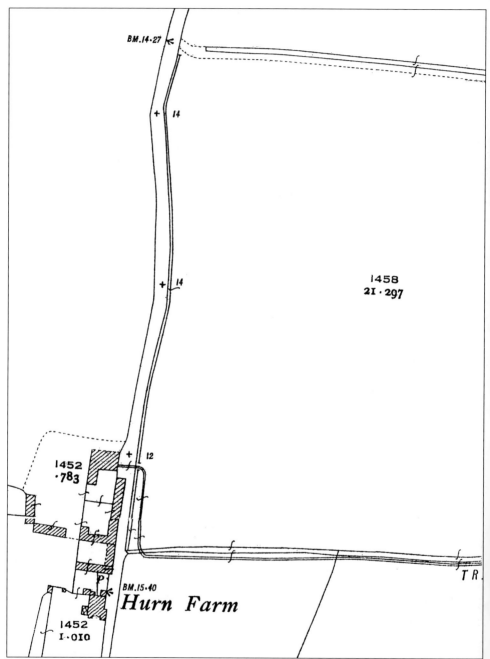

Fleet Light Railway. At Hurn Farm the line crossed the Marsh Road and ran into a farm building.
Reproduced from the 25", 1931 Edition, Ordnance Survey Map

Fleet Light Railway. A scene on the loading dock near Fleet station. The light railway wagons stand on the dock with the standard gauge trucks below to the right, into which bagged potatoes are being loaded. The simple flat wagon in the foreground has a brake handle at the far end. The gradient of the rise onto the dock can be seen in the background. *A.H. Worth & Co.*

Fleet Light Railway. A wider view of the loading dock at Fleet station about 1920. Bagged potatoes are being loaded for dispatch under the eye of the three railwaymen in the centre. There are 11 other farm workers in this view. In the far background what appear to be additional loaded wagons await their turn on the dock, probably positioned by the waiting horses. The run-round loop on the dock can be seen disappearing below their hooves. *David Spain*

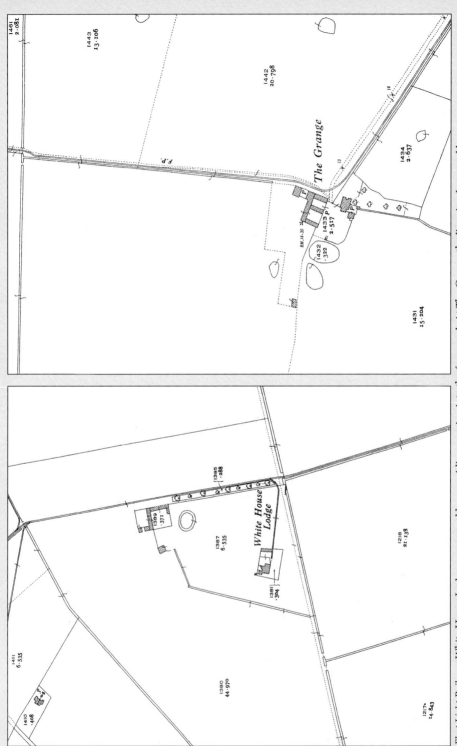

Fleet Light Railway. White House Lodge was served by one siding running into the farmyard. At The Grange the line simply passed by.

(Both) Reproduced from the 25", 1931 Edition, Ordnance Survey Map

built by Motor Rail, Works No. 5852. It has also been said that another locomotive was used, of German origin, and scrapped on site when the line closed as was No. 3759. By contrast No. 5852 was sold on to George Garside of Leighton Buzzard at that time and has survived into preservation, although, at the time of writing, is in a dismantled condition and not on show to the public. Whereas a horse could pull a maximum of about 5 tons, or four trucks loaded with up to 1½ tons each, the Simplexes could manage up to 20 tons at a time.

With the locomotive came about 10 bogie trucks with a 2½ ton capacity, a useful addition to the line's rolling stock. The normal load was about 15 tons, trains consisting of up to 12 four-wheel trucks or six bogies. Sometimes trucks became derailed on bends, the trick to overcome this being to maintain power on curves to keep the couplings taut. Rerailing was a simple matter for two men, but full trucks had to be unloaded first.

The staff to work the line consisted of three men: a driver and flagman as engine crew, and a dock porter at Fleet station. The crew did all their own maintenance on the track and rolling stock. The flagman's duties were coupling and uncoupling wagons, and protecting the train at the ungated level crossings. The train stopped a few yards short of them; the flagman stopped any traffic with a red flag in daylight, or red lamp after dark, and waited until the train was clear. This procedure also had to be followed by the crew of Thompson's trains. Little or no traffic was carried in June and so this month was devoted to track maintenance, consisting mainly of checking and putting right problems with the rails, and spreading chlorate of lime along the route to kill weeds.

A great variety of produce was carried: seed and maincrop potatoes, corn, fertiliser, celery, beans, strawberries, sugar beet, pigs, and coal for threshing machines at harvest time. All fields were numbered, and seed potato sacks were numbered accordingly to enable the crew to deliver them correctly. Shooting parties were also catered for. Piles of potato bags were placed along the sides of trucks, covered with clean sheets, for the party to sit on. A truck with a framework over it was also provided to carry the game. Field House at Fleet Hargate, now the Field House Residential Care Home, was built in 1935 for the Worth family, with all the materials taken to the site by rail.

The line was used for six days each week, taking produce to Fleet station whence it was dispatched to destinations all over the country. In the season, up to 60 tons a day, or three trainloads would be delivered. Operated without a timetable, trains could travel at up to 20 mph, usually only during the day, but after dark if it was unavoidable.

The line, because of its high standard of maintenance was usually trouble-free. The major problem, particularly after World War II, was the level crossing with the A17 in Fleet Hargate. It was crossed by up to 10 trains a day, five each way, including Thompson's trains. The growth in traffic on the road created difficulties for the flagman, particularly at dusk. On two occasions cars, failing to heed his warning, collided with trucks, but on both occasions the car drivers were found to have been drinking.

In common with other farm railways, hard roadways began to replace the line during and after World War II, and by 1952 the route mileage was down to 6¼ miles. The branches north and east of Manor House Farm were *in situ* but out

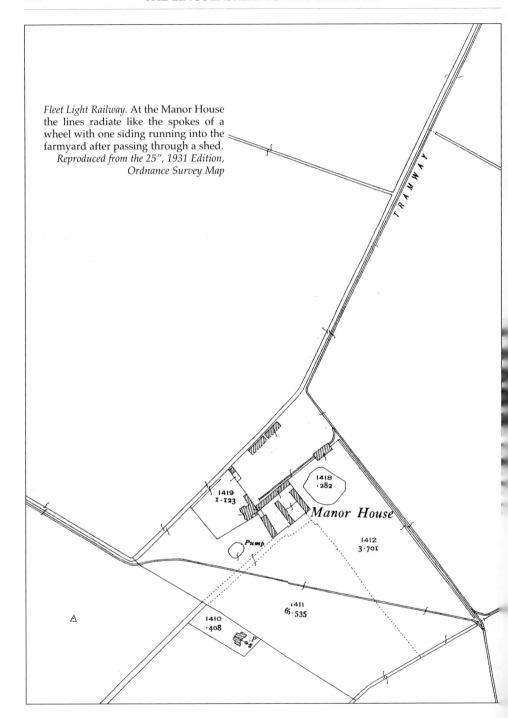

Fleet Light Railway. At the Manor House the lines radiate like the spokes of a wheel with one siding running into the farmyard after passing through a shed. *Reproduced from the 25", 1931 Edition, Ordnance Survey Map*

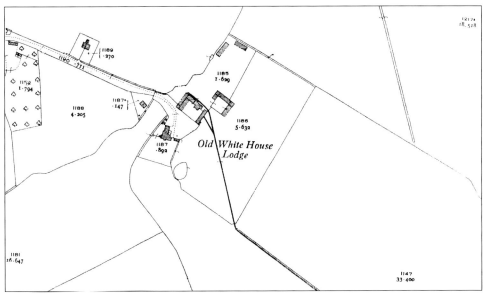

Above: Fleet Light Railway. At Old White House Lodge the line terminated as two sidings running into and alongside farm buildings.
Reproduced from the 25", 1931 Edition, Ordnance Survey Map

Left: Fleet Light Railway. The weigh machine hut from which all goods received and dispatched from the dock was weighed. Seen here in 1930. *M. Back*

Fleet Light Railway. The Light Railway closed in 1955. The dock, which still survives today although very overgrown, is seen shortly after that date. The former Midland & Great Northern Joint Railway is to the right. This line was closed to passengers on 2nd March, 1959 but the route from Spalding to Sutton Bridge, including Fleet station, remained open for goods traffic until 3rd February, 1964.   *M. Back*

Fleet Light Railway. The north side of the light railway dock, again after closure in 1955. A second siding ran along this side together with the ground level sidings which were in the foreground.
                                                                                          M. Back

of use, and the line west of The Grange was cut back. The line running northwards alongside the Fleet Haven was removed after the Dawsmere system closed in 1940. The end finally came in 1955 when the remnants were closed, and it was lifted the following year.

Virtually no trace remains today. There are some rails in a hedgerow and forming a farm gateway on the road north of Holbeach Hurn. In a nearby garden are clothes posts also from old rails. These are a mix of 20 lb. and 9 lb. per yard weight, the former predominating. This most probably is an indication that the 'main' line was laid with the heavier rail but temporary sidings into the fields, where wagons would have been pushed by man power, were of the lighter section. This would be sensible as the lighter rail was easier to handle. Many people have their memories, however, particularly of the A17 level crossing, protected for so many years by a 'black steam engine' road sign, and of a tiny train appearing, seemingly, from out of a row of houses to clatter across the road in front of them.

35. Thompson's Farm, Dawsmere

It was probably the construction of the Fleet Light Railway by Worth's which prompted J.H. Thompson, the owner of five farms around Dawsmere, to build his own line. It was built to the same nominal 2 ft gauge and had an end-on junction with the Fleet railway over which Thompson's trains ran to Fleet station. The exact date it was built is not known, it does not appear on Ordnance Survey maps of 1921, but it existed in 1927 so it was built in the early 1920s. The system, with several branches on Gedney Marsh extended for about 7‰ miles.

The line was worked both by horses, and by two diminutive diesel locomotives for all of its life. There were two bogie trucks and about 13 four-wheel trucks, some flat and some with low sides, two of which could be dropped. Each locomotive had a two-man crew who shared the driving and other tasks, including track maintenance. Some trucks could carry more than others, the smallest, 24 cwt. The normal load was six tons on five trucks, or five tons on four. All kinds of farm produce were carried, mainly potatoes and sugar beet. Pigs were also transported and for them locally-made higher sides, known as 'raves', were fitted.

The line crossed public roads at five places, two of these, over the road west of Dawsmere, were laid to fields on the south side of the road. Each field was provided with lengths of track which were laid temporarily over the surface to wherever work was taking place. A similar method was used on the Nocton Estate, but here, at Dawsmere, they were permanent level crossings serving a permanent stock of temporary track. As such they may have been unique.

The northernmost branch ran at the foot of an old sea bank, on the landward side. It was hard work to load the train with produce from the fields to the north as it all had to be manhandled over the bank.

The Fleet Light Railway has been quoted as being of 1 ft 11½ in., 1 ft 11¾ in., and 2 ft gauge. This is not surprising if track maintenance involved the measurement adopted for track repairs on this, adjacent, system. It simply involved placing the heel of one foot against one rail, and the second foot in front of the other. No wonder accurate measurement varied.

Red House Farm, Dawsmere. Pea vining in full swing in the inter-war years. A traction engine on the left is providing power for the machinery in the shed to which wagons loaded with peas have been carried. A loaded wagon waits to the left of the picture while those on the left and right in the shed are being unloaded. An empty wagon is being manhandled out of the way in the centre. This is a good illustration of how labour intensive such work was, with 10 men engaged on the task. There would probably be a further two men working on the engine.

E. Sismey

The distance from Top Farm to Fleet station was 7¼ miles, 4¼ miles of that over the Fleet Light Railway. At busy times two trains a day would run to the station, and in good weather the run would be accomplished in under an hour. It could be a different matter, however, in rain or frosty weather when much sanding of the rails would be needed.

At peak times Thompson's would run two trains each way to Fleet station. With single track and no signalling one might think the problem of two trains meeting head on would not be unusual. In practice this did not happen. Speeds were low, and visibility generally good over the flat landscape. Drivers were aware of the problem and there were many sidings and junctions where one train could wait for another to pass when spotted.

The 1940 winter was severe on the open fenland and the line was often blocked by snow. Trains were worked to a point near to Hovendon House, the goods then transhipped to a lorry, but this did not last for long as the line closed completely that February.

In its later years children from Dawsmere School used the railway to travel home at the end of their day. This was unauthorized; there was no passenger service or provision. However, this was banned after a girl fell from a truck and onto a barn door as trucks were being taken into a shed for loading.

Unusually for such lines, track survived *in situ* for over 40 years. Short lengths of rail could be found by the roadside on the first level crossing site west of Dawsmere, and that south of Holbeach St Matthew, but these had gone by the late 1990s. A brick bridge built to carry the line over a drain west of Dawsmere Bank Road still survives.

36. Red House Farm, Dawsmere

Red House Farm was the first home of George Caudwell, the pioneer of farm light railways, who lived here until moving to St Lambert's Hall, at Weston, after 1908. He built his first line at his Wraggmarsh House farm, but he followed this in the early 1920s with another, here at Red House Farm. The line was of 2 ft gauge, and horse-worked. Two miles of track radiated from the farm buildings to the north, east and west. At the ends of the permanent track sections of line were kept for laying temporary sidings across other fields.

A number of 30 cwt four-wheel trucks were provided, one horse moving 8 to 10 tons, or 5 to 7 trucks, at a time. In 1931 the railway was re-equipped with the transfer here of the wagons made redundant from the Wraggmarsh House line, when the latter was improved to enable a locomotive to be used. The local blacksmith, who had his forge at Red House Farm, carried out any maintenance on the system that could not be handled by the farm's own labour.

This is one of two lines on which it is known that the wind was used to move a truck; the other was at Leadenhall Farm. However, unlike the latter no mast was used but, with a suitable wind, two men standing up would hold a sheet between them to travel out to their work.

The line was removed shortly before World War II broke out in 1939. Sections of rail were cut up to be used both as fence posts and as reinforcing bars in the concrete floors of newer buildings.

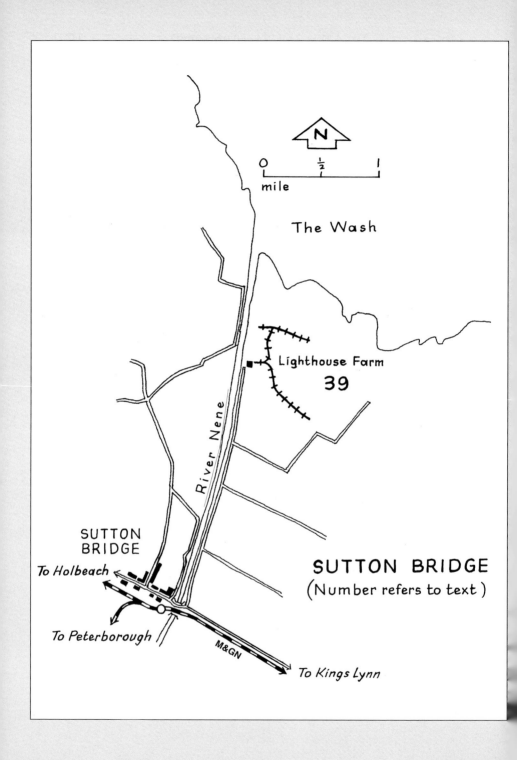

N

0 ½ 1
mile

The Wash

Lighthouse Farm
39

River Nene

SUTTON
BRIDGE

To Holbeach

SUTTON BRIDGE
(Number refers to text)

To Peterborough

M&GN

To Kings Lynn

37. Red House Farm, Gedney Dyke

On this small farm W.K. Wright used a line only ½ mile long. The date it was laid is not known and its gauge is also unrecorded. It was worked by horses; potato clamps were built alongside it and the main use was to transport bagged potatoes to the farmyard. The date the line was removed is not known but it probably did not survive after the early 1940s.

38. Brook House Farm, Gedney Dyke

A short line which existed but the route, its gauge and dates of operation are unknown. It was about ½ mile long, on land owned by the Ministry of Agriculture who let it as smallholdings. Three or four tenants used it, with horses.

39. Lighthouse Farm, Sutton Bridge

Lighthouse Farm is on land which was reclaimed from the Wash saltmarsh in the early years of the 20th century. The farmbuildings are sited near to the point where the sea bank, completed in 1910, reached the River Nene. North of this, a parallel bank was completed in 1917 and it was on this new land that a light railway was built.

In 1926 almost 1½ miles of line was constructed, running eastwards from the farmstead to form two branches of almost equal length running to the north and south. Four years later, in 1930, the northern branch was extended eastwards for a further ½ mile.

Christian & Dobbs, a Long Sutton Ironmongers and Implement Agents, who in 1926 had only recently started in business, built it (see Appendix Three). The landowner was F.K. Bass. It was horse-worked, and was of 2 ft gauge.

The line survived World War II, just, and was removed in 1946. The timber and corrugated-iron shed into which the line ran at the farmstead is still in use. Now open-sided it serves as a machinery shed. A significant amount of rail from this farm can be seen, now used as fencing, along the south boundary of the East Lighthouse, and extending across the field to the River Nene, just north of the farm. This is all of 9 lb. per yard rail, in its original five metre lengths. It is interesting that it is in metric lengths and indicates that it may well have come from France, possibly war surplus. Old rails also support the sign for the nearby Nene Lodge Farm.

40. South Fen Farm, Bourne

This farm is situated on Bourne South Fen and Northorpe Fen, three miles east of the road between Bourne and Thurlby but, to the east, bounded by the River Glen. The Glen, from its junction with the River Welland north of Spalding to the Fens south of Bourne, was navigable. Although its importance as a part of the wider waterway network had declined by the early 20th century

Lighthouse Farm. Seen in 2002 this is the former light railway shed within the farmyard. It has subsequently been converted into a machinery store with the removal of its side wall. When the railway used it the track entered from the right-hand gable. The former end door can be seen in the left-hand gable.   *Author*

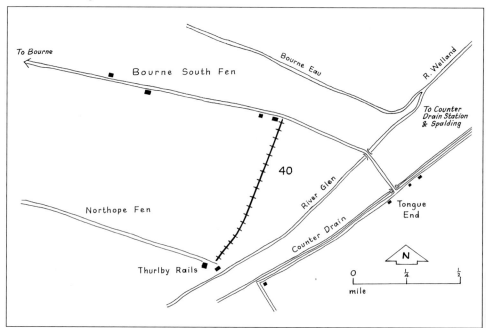

it was still in use as a link between the riverside farms and the outside world. Of particular importance was Surfleet station, on the railway line between Spalding and Boston where there was a wharf to interchange between river and rail. For this reason a farmstead had been built, Thurlby Rails, at the end of the Northorpe Fen road, alongside the River Glen.

Commercial use declined around the time of World War I and had finished by the mid-1920s. This left the farm with a problem. The north side lay along a road that ran through the fen to a bridge over the River Glen. This gave good road links with Bourne and Spalding as well as Counter Drain railway station between the two. The south end of the farm, including Thurlby Rails Farm, was now isolated within the Fen. Only ⁷⁄₁₀ mile, three fields, away from the road to the north it was no less than seven miles away by road.

The answer was to link the two by a light railway and this was done in the mid-1920s. The farm was owned, at that time, by R.K. Watts. The line was used by horses but the date it was closed and other details are unknown.

41. Tongue End Farm, Deeping St Nicholas

Any link between the Tongue End Farm railway and the British Empire Exhibition at Wembley in 1924 would seem very tenuous, but there was one. The Exhibition, for which Wembley Stadium was one of the buildings, was opened by King George V on St George's Day, 1924. It was a 220-acre extravaganza demonstrating all that was then modern, and illustrating the multitudinous aspects of life and geography throughout the Empire. One of its lesser-known features was what was called the 'Never Stop' Railway. This was a narrow gauge railway that ran around the site and, literally, never stopped. The train of open-sided carriages only slowed down at the stations, slow enough to enable passengers to enter and leave. After the Exhibition closed it was, along with the rest of the site and many of the buildings, dismantled and put up for sale. Sold piecemeal, mostly for scrap, it disappeared, but one coach was purchased by F.H. Cooke, of Town End Manor, Spalding, who owned Tongue End Farm, and used for his personal pleasure on this, his farm railway.

This must have been quite an undertaking for such a farm railway. Eight 'Neverstop Railway' carriages were bought by the Ashover Light Railway for their 2 ft gauge line in Derbyshire. They were delivered, as Mr Cooke's would have been, with rubber-tyred wheels with no flanges. These had run on a concrete track, the train driven by an arm from the carriage underframe clamping on to a shaft with a spiral threaded constantly rotating shaft running along the route. This was the 'Adkins-Lewis Rapid Varying Speed Continuous Transport System'. The coaches at Ashover had their underframes and wheels removed and replaced by bogies taken from ex-WD wagons. A similar conversion would have to have been undertaken at Tongue End Farm. This may not have been as difficult as it may seem at first impression. It was not unusual in Lincolnshire for farm railway track and equipment to be laid, maintained and adapted by farm labour. Engineering skills had been one of the abilities of farm workers and those trades who serve them for many years.

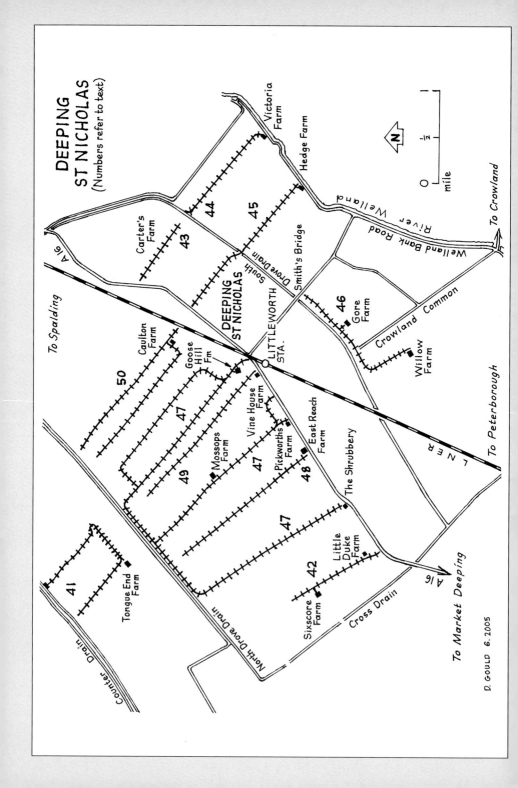

The line was built in 1923 or 1924, and ran for almost 2½ miles around the farm, with both termini adjacent to the road which runs from Spalding to Boston. Six bogie trucks were supplied and initially horses moved them around. The rails ran through a greenhouse in which the potatoes, the main product of the farm, were chitted.

In the 1930s Mr Cooke formed a partnership with a Hugh Chatterton, to form a company called Chatterton and Cooke. It was Chatterton who, believing a locomotive would be a useful addition to the line, built a small petrol motor. It had no gears, other than forward and reverse, and was capable of hauling up to three trucks loaded with up to five tons, similar to the farm horses.

The line was closed and taken up immediately after World War II, but some track and equipment was relaid on a bulb farm at Pinchbeck, where for a few years more it was used to move boxes of bulbs around a number of glasshouses.

42. Sixscore and Little Duke Farms, Deeping St Nicholas

A small system, of about 1³⁄₁₀ miles, which appears to have been built in the late 1920s, Sixscore Farm was sold by a Mr O. Flint in 1934, and the line was certainly *in situ* at that time. Horses worked the line; its gauge is unrecorded. In 1934 the farm was sold to E.D. and A.D. Cooke who continued to use it until the eve of World War II. It was probably, therefore, one of the shortest-lived lines, existing for only about 10 years.

Sixscore Farm used six flat trucks, one of which was fitted with a handbrake. There were two more trucks on the system, owned by R.W. Grooby of Little Duke Farm. The line ran alongside the present day farm road before crossing it on the approach to the main road where it ran up onto a loading dock. This dock, and the bend in the line on its approach, made the railway a particularly good playground for children, the slope from the dock ensured that a truck would take the bend at an exhilarating speed.

43. Carter's Farm, Deeping St Nicholas

The land on which this line ran was farmed by A.H. Carter from about 1910 to 1980. Its construction is believed to date from the late 1920s, the gauge is not known. At about ⁹⁄₁₀ mile it was one of the smallest railways. Horse-worked, it had about four small trucks. There was a loading dock adjacent to the main road.

It was one of two lines in this area to survive the war, although it was taken out of use around 1950. Some rails survive as fence posts around a paddock at White House Farm nearby.

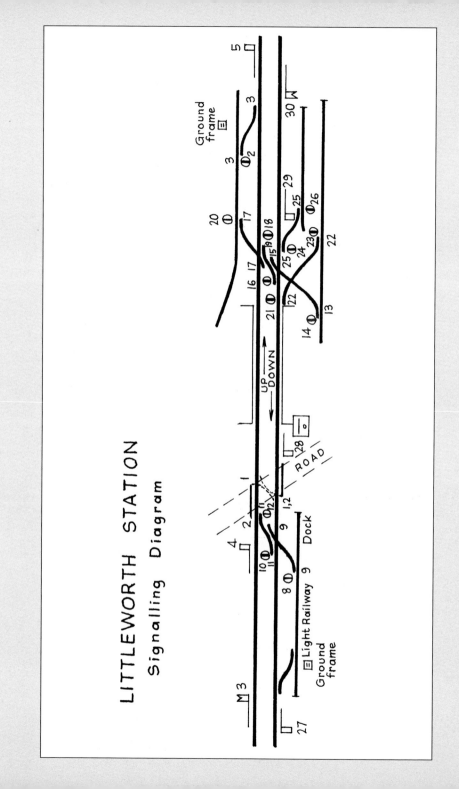

LITTLEWORTH STATION
Signalling Diagram

44. Victoria Farm, Deeping St Nicholas

A 1¾₀ mile line was built on this farm about 1925, gauge not known. The farm produced mainly grain and potatoes. For most of its life horses provided the motive power, but in its final years a tractor was used. It was taken out of use in the period 1948/1950.

This is one of the farms where rail lengths were cut up to form fence posts and some of these can be seen today, both from Deeping High Bank, the road that runs alongside the River Welland, as well as the minor road from Deeping High Bank along the northern boundary of the farm.

45. Hedge Farm, Deeping St Nicholas

This 2 mile-long line was operating in 1918, its gauge is not known. Up to 1924, the farm was owned by Mr W.E. Porter, then being sold to a Mr Richardson. The sleepers were bought second-hand and were a constant source of trouble, the track requiring frequent maintenance. There were 12 trucks, some of 2 tons capacity, others 30 cwt. The 2 ton trucks had head and tailboards. One horse could haul three trucks, one 2 ton vehicle usually sandwiched between two smaller ones. A double bend at the half-way stage was always a problem and, despite each truck being taken through them individually, derailments were frequent. This occasionally meant loads being dropped into the drains! At the northern end were a small transhipment shed and a loading dock.

The railway survived in use up to 1944, and was dismantled in 1946.

46. Bottom Farm, Crowland

Known as the Bottom Farm system, and built before 1928, the 1¾ miles of line served Willow Farm at its southern end, with a short branch to Core Farm at about the half-way mark. The eastern terminus was adjacent to the Deeping St Nicholas to Crowland road, on the south side of Smith's Bridge over the South Drove Drain. Gore Farm eastwards was on land farmed by W. Dennis & Sons, the rest on land farmed by a Mr Watts. It is believed to have been of 2 ft gauge. It was horse-worked and about six trucks were in use. The system was taken out of use about 1935.

47. Dennis Estates, Deeping St Nicholas

W. Dennis & Sons cultivated some 2,000 acres of land on Deeping Fen, growing mainly potatoes. In 1910 they established a 2 ft gauge light railway from their private sidings adjacent to the Spalding to Peterborough railway, at Littleworth station, serving much of their Estate. It grew to have a total of 20 miles, as reported in the press at the time. The route mileage, from contemporary maps and peoples memories, appears to have been about 11 miles. This is a big discrepancy which can be accounted for only partly by sidings and lengths of temporary track to serve

Dennis Estates, Deeping St Nicholas. An interesting comparison between the narrow and standard gauge locomotives. LNER 'J3' class 0-6-0 No. 4109, stands in the private siding north of Littleworth station on 21st April, 1926. Alongside is the LIFU locomotive used by Dennis Estates between 1924 and 1926 with a healthy load of bagged potatoes. *Author's Collection*

Dennis Estates, Deeping St Nicholas. The LIFU locomotive of Dennis Estates stands on the loading dock at Littleworth on 21st April, 1926. Seven open wagons have been loaded with bagged potatoes. *Author's Collection*

fields for a short time during planting or harvest only. The farms served were Goose Hill Farm, Pickworth's Farm and The Shrubbery. At Goose Hill Farm there were a number of sidings serving, among other buildings, a large glasshouse. The *Light Railway and Tramway Journal*, on 15th April, 1910, reported:

> The example set by Alderman Worth, at Holbeach Hurn, of the construction of a light railway connecting up his farms with the main line railway, has been followed at Littleworth, where Messrs W. Dennis & Sons have linked up their farms in Deeping Fen, Lincs, by a line of this character, which is only now waiting to be connected to the trunk line at the station. It will, like Mr Worth's pioneer line, be worked by horse traction, but even so, an enormous economy is effected over road haulage.

In addition to being the longest of the light railways on Deeping Fen, it also had a connection to the national railway network. To the north of Littleworth station level crossing, a private siding ran alongside a loading dock about 100 yards long; the narrow gauge track ran up a ramp onto this to enable transhipment from one system to the other. In common with other such loading docks at Fleet and Nocton sidings also ran parallel at ground level for loading down from the standard to the narrow gauge. The standard gauge siding consisted of a loop off the down main line.

Twenty to 30 flat trucks were used on the line, each capable of carrying two tons. They appear to have been used in rakes of up to five.

Horsepower was always used on the line, but until 1926 an LIFU steam tractor was also used. The date it was delivered is not known but it was photographed here in 1916. This was of an unusual design; its inspiration appeared to be the early steam cars which appeared on the roads in the early years of the century. It had a paraffin-fired boiler with a car bonnet over it. Out of this grew the chimney. The driver sat on a bench seat behind the bonnet and behind him was a flat platform body, which could be loaded. However, it proved to be too heavy for the track, either because the track foundations were not adequate, or the sleepers rotted quickly. Either could apply as in those days the water table was high in winter months. For more detail see Chapter Six.

In the mid-1920s the connection alongside the North Drove Drain from Pickworth's Farm to a point just over one mile north of The Shrubbery was removed, together with the loop line on Goose Hill Farm. This gave two lines independently operated, just over one mile from The Shrubbery, and an inverted 'U'-shaped system of about 5½ miles from the main road at Pickworth's Farm, to Littleworth station, via North Drove Drain. In about 1928, the remaining stretch alongside the North Drove Drain was removed, leaving three separate systems.

The Shrubbery line was the first of these to close, in 1930, Pickworth's Farm closed around the time of World War II, and, finally, Goose Hill Farm in 1950. The warehouse for the loading dock survives today and can still be seen to the north of the level crossing at Deeping St Nicholas.

Dennis Estates, Deeping St Nicholas. This is a view of Goose Hill Farm, near to Littleworth station, in 1916. Alongside the farm buildings is the glasshouse used for chitting potatoes. This could hold 200 to 250 tons. Narrow gauge wagons of bagged potatoes can be seen in the background with the line's LIFU locomotive, with a short train, in the foreground.   *Railway Magazine*

Dennis Estates, Deeping St Nicholas. The potato warehouse at Littleworth station was situated alongside the standard gauge siding on the down side of the line. More bagged potatoes are awaiting dispatch. Outside the warehouse the narrow gauge siding is on a level with the main line. The loading dock was to the north or right-hand side. This photograph was taken in 1916.
Railway Magazine

48. East Reach Farm, Deeping St Nicholas

Before 1914, almost two miles of line, running north-west as straight as an arrow, was built from East Reach Farm alongside the Spalding to Peterborough main road, for the farmer, Sydney Worth. The gauge is not recorded, it was horse-worked.

The farm was later bought by the County Council and partitioned into smallholdings. Four tenants used the line who had one truck each. The northern half was taken up in 1940 and sold, so local rumour has it, to be melted down for munitions. The remainder did not survive the war and was removed, probably in the mid-1940s.

49. Vine House Farm, Deeping St Nicholas

Almost two miles of track, described as being about 2 ft 2 in. gauge, was laid on this farm as a single straight line from the farmstead out on to the Fen. The date it was built is not known, but it went out of use during World War II. It was horse-worked with four flat trucks. A horse would pull one truck at a time because, although the land appeared to be level, silt hills rising to about six to eight feet precluded a greater load.

In winter the horse would walk on the sleepers to gain purchase but on occasions its steel shod hooves would slip causing the truck to run into the horse. The horseshoes also damaged the sleepers. When the land was dry the horse walked alongside the track and these problems did not occur.

A timber loading dock, typical of this Fen, was built in the farmyard from the top of which the truck would be unloaded into a horsedrawn road wagon for the short journey to Littleworth station. The loading dock still survives in a field at the rear of the farmyard, as do short lengths of rail in the rafters of one of the farm buildings on the site.

50. Caulton Farm, Deeping St Nicholas

This farm is also known as Worth's Farm. The railway was built about 1921, there being two linked branches, running from the farmstead north-westwards onto the Fen. It had a total length of about 3¾₀ miles. It is likely that the eastern branch was constructed first, with the western one following after 1928. Trucks were hauled by horses, potatoes and mustard being the principal crops.

The eastern branch remained in use until about 1950, but the other branch, and their connecting link, had closed prior to this date.

Vine House Farm, Deeping St Nicholas. The farm loading dock in a dilapidated condition in 1986.
Author

Vine House Farm, Deeping St Nicholas. The restored loading dock today, now with rails and a wagon.
Author

Chapter Six

The Dennis Locomotives

On their estates W. Dennis & Sons used a variety of types of locomotive: petrol, diesel and steam at Nocton and a very unusual steam locomotive at Deeping St James. The individual details of each of the petrol and diesel and steam locomotives which ran at Nocton are set out in *Table Six*. A total of 11 locomotives were used.

Motor Rail and Tramcar Ltd (MRT) and Motor Rail Ltd (MR) of Bedford marketed their locomotives under the trade name 'Simplex'. T.D. Abbott designed their 20 hp and 40 hp engines for military use, during 1916. They were an extremely successful design and 590 were built for the War Department. Some of the larger version were fully armoured with a curved steel shield. At one side sat the driver facing sideways, for driving in either direction, at the other was the radiator. The Dixon-Abbott gearbox gave similar speeds in either direction. It was to this company that W. Dennis & Sons turned to provide motive power for their new railway. It is of interest that some of the administration of the Nocton Estate was carried out from the Kirton office, as the locomotive orders for the first, un-numbered, Simplex, and for Nos. 1 to 4, were issued from there.

The first locomotive, possibly MRT 1952 of 1919, arrived for trials in 1920. This was returned to the manufacturer in the same year. At 6 tons it proved too heavy for the track. Orders were subsequently placed for lighter machines from the same manufacturer. Three of the 2½ ton 20 hp model were delivered in 1920, Works No. 1935 in January, No. 1938 in February and No. 1440 in March. At Nocton, these were numbered 1, 2 and 3. A fourth locomotive from the same manufacturer followed in 1923, and numbered 4. The latter was heavier than its predecessors, at 4 tons, and had a straight-sided frame. All the lighter Simplexes used at Nocton had bow frames. All four had a 20 hp 2-cylinder, transverse, water-cooled, petrol engine driving a gear box providing two speeds in both directions.

In 1926 Messrs John Fowler & Co. of Leeds supplied a steam locomotive to Nocton. It has been said that they did use a second steam locomotive but this is something of a mystery. *The Locomotive*, 15th November, 1926, describes the Fowler engine and refers only to 'small petrol locomotives' being used prior to its delivery in that year. However, the Industrial Locomotive Society has heard that during the Dennis ownership an 0-4-0 saddle tank with outside cylinders and a small boiler was used. This was from a Hunslet manufacturer and, after a short time, was returned to them. The boiler size required it to stop regularly to raise steam. At Nocton it had been known as 'Rocket'.

One other possible suggestion can be offered. From before 1916 until 1926 a small steam tractor was used on the Dennis Estate at Deeping St Nicholas. It may have been that this was tried out at Nocton prior to its disposal. Having said that, it certainly would not have been capable of carrying out the work that the Fowler was acquired for and this would have been known prior to any trial.

The locomotive at Deeping St Nicholas was a LIFU steam lorry. This was one of a small number made by the Liquid Fuel Company on the Isle of Wight. The

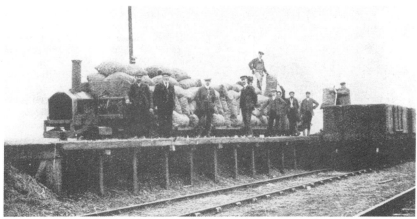

Dennis Estates, Deeping St Nicholas. Transhipping sacks of potatoes from the light railway into wagons in the Dennis private siding at Littleworth in 1916.   *Railway Magazine*

principle was a flash steam boiler that could be ready for use very quickly by spraying paraffin on to a hot surface. This drove one pair of wheels and was permanently coupled to a trailer. It looked like a road lorry on rails which was not surprising as road versions were also made.

Little is known about the total numbers produced or where they were used. One is known to have been used on another farm railway, in Ireland. This was at Kildysart in County Clare on the farm of John O'Connell Bianconi. A description of its operation has survived:

> There were twelve coils in front of the cab and a burner underneath with fourteen jets. The burner started with methylated spirits and when it was warm a supply of paraffin was turned to steam and when the gauge got to 50lb you were ready to go.

Given the levels of production here extensive use must have been used of horses for prime motive power, as it became exclusively after 1926. No photograph shows a name or number being carried. However, it was known as 'Billy', presumably after William Dennis.

It is believed that the Nocton Estate used a number of Fowler steam traction engines and it may be for that reason that they turned to John Fowler & Co. for their steam railway locomotive. This had some unusual features for a locomotive operating in Great Britain in that it had a spark arrestor chimney and a water lifter to enable the side tanks to be filled from any handy drain. The latter was particularly useful in an area like the Nocton and Dunston fens where piped water was non-existent but water in drains was plentiful.

As stated above, in 1926 *The Locomotive* carried a description of the Fowler locomotive recently supplied to the Nocton Estate. This said,

> Up to the introduction of the present steam locomotive, the potatoes have been hauled on a light railway by means of small petrol locomotives, but on the main line to the

station there is a gradient of about 1 in 40 about half a mile long, over which the petrol locomotives have been able only to haul very small loads.

The engine, of the 0-6-0 type, is designed for the 60-centimetre gauge. It has 8 in. diameter cylinders with a piston stroke of 12 in. The wheelbase is 5 ft. and the diameter of the wheels is 24 in. The tank has a capacity for 250 gallons of water and the fuel bunker space is 15 cu. ft. The working boiler pressure is 180 lb. per square inch. The heating surface comprises 28 sq. ft. from the firebox and 242 sq. ft from the tubes, making a total heating surface of 270 sq. ft.; the grate area is 5 sq. ft.

The actual weight of the locomotive empty is 9 tons 7 cwt, and in working order 11 tons 15 cwt.; the tractive effort is 4,320 lb. The engine will haul 204 tons on the level, 128 tons up a gradient of 1 in 200 and 94 tons up a gradient of 1 in 100. It will haul 50 tons up the gradient of 1 in 40 even on badly laid rails. The minimum weight of rails used is 20 lb. per yard; the radius of the sharpest curve traversed is 80 ft. The locomotive is fitted with a water lifter so that it can draw its own supplies from the river running through the estate.

Despite the optimistic words about how it would perform even on badly laid rails its performance did not come up to expectations. Too heavy for the fenland rails, west of Wasps Nest it tended to spread the rails on curves, again because of its weight. It spent much of its time languishing in its shed adjacent to the mill at Nocton. It was sold about 1930 to George Cohen & Sons of Leeds. It was subsequently used in County Durham for the construction of Burnhope Reservoir near Cowshill in Upper Weardale. When this contract was completed it was one of two steam locomotives offered for sale in the *Contract Journal*, 27th January, 1937, by George Cohen & Sons of Stanningley Plant Depot, Leeds. They must have been acting as agents for the sale as, on 2nd June, 1937, it was one of nine 2 ft gauge steam locomotives advertised by the Durham County Water Board, all which could be inspected on site. It is believed that it was scrapped on site, in 1938.

Why such a heavy locomotive was purchased given that trials with a six-ton locomotive had been tried before and found too heavy is difficult to understand. It may be that it was felt that the levels of track maintenance were higher than before. It certainly seems likely, given the subsequent expansion of the fleet, that additional motive power was needed. Whatever the reason steam power was not tried again.

Ruston & Hornsby Ltd (RH), of Lincoln, began building locomotives in 1931. Their first design was a 10 hp production of which started in 1931. Their second was the 16 hp which had a Lister engine. This was a class of 56 locomotives, all built in 1932/33/34. By the time their last locomotive rolled off the production line in February 1969 the firm had built more diesel locomotives than any other British manufacturer. Perhaps thinking that they should support a local company and/or from which they might get a good deal, it was to Ruston's that Dennis's turned next.

Ruston RH 165365 was the first of its type and delivered to Nocton in March 1932. RH 166018 came, also new, in 1933. It is believed that they were not in use at the same time. Ruston's, ever mindful of the need for good photographs showing their new locomotives at work, took publicity photographs of RH 165365 at work at Nocton and used them in their staff magazine and early brochures.

The Ruston engines were not popular. The plate clutch needed regular adjustment and the sanding of the rails on the gradients off the Fens was inadequate. Both stayed only a very short time and both had gone by the end of 1933.

It was probably as a result of using these oil-engined locomotives that the Estate decided to replace the petrol engines on their existing Simplexes with diesels. The work was done in the Estate workshops, three in 1934 and the other two years later. The replacements were all Dorman Diesel units. At the same time wooden cabs were fitted to give the drivers protection from the elements. An additional Simplex, Works No. MRT 3995, was added to the fleet in March 1934.

The Estate was sold to Smith's Potato Crisps in 1936 and it was they who added the final locomotive, in September 1950. This was yet another diesel-engined Simplex, Works No. 3652. This was a rebuild of a petrol-engined locomotive, Works No. 1677, of 1918. It was delivered new to the West Riding County Council in 1925. It came to Nocton, in its later guise, from S. Toulson of Knottingley in West Yorkshire.

No. 4 was converted to a snowplough after 1936. No. 5 was sold to the Lincolnshire Coast Light Railway in May 1960. Nos. 2, 3 and 6 were sold for scrap about September 1960 and were removed from the estate. Finally, when the last vestige of the railway was closed No. 1 followed No. 5, in September 1969, to the Lincolnshire Coast Light Railway.

Table Six
Locomotive Fleet, Nocton Estate Light Railway

No.	Type	Works No.	Class	Weight	Notes
-	4wPM	MRT 1952 (?)	40 hp	6 t.	New ex-works on trial 1920. Returned MRT by 26/3/1920. Subsequently sold to Marshall Sons & Co. (India) Ltd of Bombay.
1	4wPM	MRT 1935	20 hp	2½ t.	New ex-works 13/1/1920. Converted 4wDM 4/1934. To LCLR 7/1969.
2	4wPM	MRT 1938	20 hp	2½ t.	New ex-works 11/2/1920. Converted 4wDM 1934.
3	4wPM	MRT 1440	20 hp	2½ t	New ex-works 9/3/1920. Converted 4wDM 6/1936.
4	4wPM	MRT 2083	20 hp	4 t.	New ex-works 18/11/1923. Converted 4wDM 5/1934. Converted to snow plough after 1936.
-	0-6-0T	JF 16991	-	9 t. 7 cwt	New ex-works 1926. Sold to Durham County Water Board by 6/1934.
-	4wDM	RH 165365	16 hp	2¾ t.	New ex-works 3/1932. Disposed of 1933. Subsequently sold to Curral, Lewis & Martin, Contractors, by 1937.
-	4w DM	RH 166018	16 hp	2¾ t.	New ex-works 1/1933. Sold 1933 to J.C. Rodgers & Sons, Castleford.
5	4wDM	MR 3995	20/28 hp	2½ t.	Reconditioned and ex-works 6/3/1934. To LCLR 5/1960.
6	4wDM	MRT3652	20 hp	2½ tons	New to West Riding County Council 2/5/1924. Acquired by Nocton Estate 9/1950.

MRT	Motor Rail and Tramcar Ltd	RH	Ruston & Hornsby Ltd
MR	Motor Rail Ltd	LCLR	Lincolnshire Coast Light Railway
JF	John Fowler & Co		

Chapter Seven

The Nocton Rolling Stock

This Chapter looks in some detail at the history of the ex-War Department rolling stock used at Nocton. Many railways equipped themselves after the Great War with such material. Many of these were in India and Argentina. Some were used on light railways in Great Britain where two in particular were new lines utilising almost exclusively ex-WD stock, the Ashover Light Railway and at Nocton. The particular interest of the former Nocton stock lies in that some was bought by the Lincolnshire Coast Light Railway. Some were subsequently sold to other parts of the preservation movement. Over the years much has been scrapped or used for spares. Others have been rebuilt. However, a few precious examples have survived largely unaltered to be the only surviving examples of their type.

Class 'D'

This was the most common wagon produced for the War Department. Designed in 1916, they were bogie open wagons with a 10 ton capacity and were designed to carry road making materials and ammunition. Each side had two drop down doors, with a removable centre post in between, to make unloading quick and easy. They were just over 20 feet long over the buffers with a body width of 5 ft 2½ in., and a length of 17 ft 8½ in. They weighed a little over two tons. Some had a steel underframe, others timber. Clayton & Shuttleworth of Lincoln manufactured some of the former for the War Department. They had a hand brake on a pillar rising at the ends from each bogie although at Nocton contemporary photographs show them as only running with one. The Estate had its own workshops and modified all rolling stock to its own need as necessary so this may have been a local modification. They were easily recognisable as the underframe formed an elongated V shape in elevation.

Class 'E'

This class was also a bogie wagon with the same dimensions as the class 'D'. The main difference was that they had a steel frame forming a well below the body and the body had a single central drop down door on either side. They were designed to carry light but bulky loads such as timber and hay fodder for horses. Both this and the class 'D' could be converted to carry wounded on stretchers with the provision of a canvas awning.

The Nocton Estate took delivery of 53 wagons of a mix of class 'D' and 'E'. Judging solely from the evidence of surviving photographs class 'D' appears to have been the most numerous. The underframe of one of the latter was used for the Nocton coach and two others were converted to form the oil train, carrying

Nocton Estate. In 1932 the local locomotive manufacturer, Ruston's of Lincoln, supplied one of their products. They began making locomotives in 1931 and this 16 hp 4w DM, Works No. 165365, came for testing. Ruston's took the opportunity to take publicity photographs for their catalogue and this was taken on 8th November, 1932. The train is standing, with an impressive load, immediately east of the level crossing over the Sleaford road, north of the Estate Yard. The wagons appear to be being operated as two sets of two. This is the only photograph where wagons are numbered in this way. That next to the locomotive, numbered 41, is a former WD class 'E', the others, class 'D'. *Ray Hooley*

Nocton Estate. Here potatoes are being removed from the straw-covered grave and loaded into two former WD ambulance vans. These vans were limited to a load of about three tons. They could carry more but were prone to overturn if the load shifted on some of the sharp curves. This is a good illustration of how the railway ran along the field edge serving the fields on either side. The photograph was taken in 1937. *Institute of Agricultural History*

diesel fuel and paraffin, used to take fuel out to the early tractors and supply the isolated farm houses with their domestic needs.

After closure four, one class 'E' and three class 'D', were sold to the Festiniog Railway. One of these, Smith's No. 18, Festiniog No. 60, was subsequently scrapped. Two, Smith's Nos. 31 and 9, Festiniog Nos. 61 and 62 respectively, have been converted to fuel tankers. The class 'E', Smith's No. 3, Festiniog No. 63, still survives in regular use. All four were built by Robert Hudson Ltd of Leeds.

Nine or ten class 'D' were sold at various dates to the Lincolnshire Coast Light Railway. This was being established at Humberston, south of Cleethorpes, in 1960. Some were converted to open coaches, others were dismantled and their bogies used to restore the Nocton coach and the former Ashover Light Railway coaches the line had also acquired. Two remained in original condition. These were repainted in their original colour scheme and were on display in the Museum of Army Transport in Beverley for some years. No longer there, they are now in the care of the Lincolnshire Coast Light Railway. The Gloucester Railway Carriage & Wagon Works built both of these examples.

Class 'H'

This was a water tank wagon with a 1,500 gallon steel tank mounted on a 'D' class underframe. Used to transport water for both men and animals behind the front line they had a filler cap at either end. Water was an important commodity to be transported at Nocton also and they continued to provide their valuable service in Lincolnshire. After closure the tanks were removed from their frames and placed around the Estate yard to hold water for firefighting use in an emergency. One of them is still there today.

Ambulance Vans

These, all built in 1917 and 1918, were for carrying wounded men back from near the front lines. They had fittings for carrying eight stretcher cases and a bench for four walking wounded. The fittings could be removed for use as covered vans for other purposes. The body was 20 ft 6 in. long, 6 ft wide and with 6 ft 3 in. headroom in the centre. They had central double doors on either side, some sliding and others hinged, with sliding doors in their ends to enable staff to pass from one to another on the move.

Nocton acquired 12 of these. Again, surviving photographs show only those with sliding doors. They were not popular at Nocton as they were very unstable when loaded. Sacks of potatoes often fell against the doors in transit and prevented them from being slid open. At least one was modified by the Estate with side-hinged doors. The Lincolnshire Coast Light Railway subsequently acquired two. They intended to convert them to passenger coaches but their acquisition of the Ashover Light Railway coaches meant that they were not needed. One was used as a travelling waiting room and ticket office, to be placed at the far end of the line each day the railway was running and was also used for passengers on Sunday

Market trains in the 1970s. It was sold on to the South Tynedale Railway at Alston in Cumbria and used as a tool storage van when the railway was being built and then as a stationary shed in the Works Yard. Dismantled for rebuilding, it has since been sold and is not on public display. The other was put on display with other vehicles at the Museum of Army Transport but has since been removed and is currently with the Lincolnshire Coast Light Railway.

Class 'P'

These were four-wheel ration wagons, built from 1917 on, some by Clayton & Shuttleworth of Lincoln. With lattice timber sides they weighed less than a ton. They were designed to be able to run on poorly laid track so they could penetrate almost to the front line, here pushed by hand. Further back, on track capable of supporting engines, they could be formed into trains.

Nocton acquired 36 of these. Here, many were fitted with plank sides and used to carry sand and track ballast. Others were converted to brakevans.

At least six were sold to the Lincolnshire Coast Light Railway. Two have been scrapped and another moved to the Amberley Chalk Pits Museum in Sussex where it has been restored to its original appearance. Three remain at Winthorpe, one rebuilt to a Class 'Q'.

Class 'Q'

These were a slightly larger version of the class 'P'. It is not known how many were at Nocton but one has survived, rebuilt from a class 'P', and fitted with plank sides, to become part of the stock of the Lincolnshire Coast Light Railway.

Tip Wagons

There were an unspecified number of these four-wheeled wagons at Nocton. They may have been ex-WD class 'K' tip wagons of a conventional design, with a V-shaped metal body which could be tipped to one side for emptying. None of them survived into preservation.

Preservation

Four of the wagons from Nocton are in the care of The Lincolnshire Coast Light Railway Historical Vehicles Trust, established in 1983. These have been restored to their original condition as used by the Army in World War I and comprise an ambulance van, a 'D' class bogie open wagon, a 'D' class flat bogie wagon and a class 'P' ration wagon. For a time these were on display at the Museum of Army Transport at Beverley but now are housed with the Lincolnshire Coast Light Railway at Winthorpe.

Chapter Eight

Potato Railways - The Successors

Although all of the farm railways in the County are now long gone there are a few places in Lincolnshire where the narrow gauge lives on and where a flavour of what the lines must have been like can be gained.

Lincolnshire Coast Light Railway

In 1958 a group of narrow gauge enthusiasts in north Lincolnshire were determined that the area should have its own railway. Taking advantage of the closure of the Nocton railway in 1960 they purchased 700 yards of track, one Simplex locomotive, Nocton No. 5, two bogie ex-WD ambulance vans, two bogie and five four-wheeled wagons. In 1969 another locomotive, Nocton No. 1, five bogie wagons and one four-wheeled wagon followed. With these, and track and other equipment from other sources, the Lincolnshire Coast Light Railway was created (*see Chapters Six and Seven for further details*).

In 1960 the railway acquired a site at North Sea Lane at Humberston on the southern outskirts of Cleethorpes. It was envisaged from the start that the line should serve a public transport need and link the southern terminus of the Cleethorpes and Grimsby bus services with a number of holiday camps built behind the beach. Some 700 yards of track was laid between North Sea Lane, the main base, to a smaller station, named Beach, at the entrance of the first of the camps. It opened on 27th August, 1960 and provided a service in the summer months and at the Easter and Whitsun Bank Holidays.

In 1966 a new line was built, almost a mile in extent, alongside the original but extending further south at the far end to a new terminus, South Sea Lane. This opened on 15th August, 1966.

To work their services the railway acquired equipment from a variety of sources and has become the owner of a number of historically important vehicles. The Nocton coach had been sold to a scrap yard in Sleaford who used it as an office and that came to them, together with a coach from the Sand Hutton Light Railway and two coaches from the Ashover Light Railway. The latter were given ex-Nocton 'D' class bogies to enable them to run again. Two ex-Nocton timber-framed bogie wagons were utilised to provide the underframe for the Sand Hutton coach, each shortened and joined to suit the length. The latter had timber underframes built originally by the Gloucester Railway Carriage & Wagon Company.

A number of additional Simplex locomotives and a steam locomotive, *Jurassic*, an 0-6-0 built by Peckett & Sons for the Southam Limeworks of Kaye & Company Ltd, of 1903, were used in addition to the former Nocton engines.

The railway closed after the 1985 season and was lifted in 1987. The collection was, however, kept together and is now at a holiday camp and leisure park at Winthorpe near Skegness. Not yet open to the public, several hundred yards of

Lincolnshire Coast Light Railway. Two feet gauge track, spiked to timber sleepers, running alongside the fields, was very typical of many Lincolnshire farm railways.   *Author*

Lincolnshire Coast Light Railway. The Nocton coach in 2005, awaiting restoration.   *Author*

Lincolnshire Coast Light Railway. One of the ex Nocton bogie wagons now restored to its original WD condition, part of the historic collection of vehicles based on the railway. This wagon was built by the Gloucester Railway Carriage & Wagon Co. Ltd, in Gloucester. *Author*

track has been laid, including some lengths ex-Nocton, and a storage shed built with the aim of reopening in the future.

Amongst the ex-Nocton items in their care are a section of track and a 'D' class wagon, the latter converted to an open coach to run in the opening train at Humberston in August 1960, which both show shrapnel damage from World War I. They also provide a base for the four ex-WD wagons now restored to their World War I appearance in the care of the Lincolnshire Coast Light Railway Historical Vehicles Trust.

North Ings Farm Railway

North Ings Farm is situated on the edge of the fens two miles east of the village of Dorrington, between Lincoln and Sleaford and is owned and farmed by T.W.F. Hall. The railway here was laid in 1972 specifically to provide access around the farm which, at that time, was used for rearing chickens. The first equipment came from the Whisby gravel pit of Robert Teal Ltd, and consisted of an 'LBT' class Ruston diesel locomotive, Works No. RH 371937, two skips and 50 yards of 2 ft gauge track.

The line was an immediate success and the decision was made to extend it. The following year additional track was purchased from the Nene River Board and from the Nocton Estate. Worked as a private line, as it became known it began to attract the occasional visitors and additional engines and wagons were acquired from time to time.

In 1981 the production of chickens and eggs became uneconomic and this element of the work ceased. The development of a trout lake on the farm required an extension of the line. Track and rolling stock came from the Escrick Tile Works near York and rail and points from the Goxhill Tileries on the bank of the River Humber. Additional locomotives came from a variety of sources.

Pinchbeck Bulb Museum. Grass grown track looking as it must have done on so many farm railways in the County. The turntable in the background is a feature more common within nurseries in the fens of Lincolnshire. These enabled a grid of rails to be laid to serve beds within nurseries where wagons were pushed manually and speeds were very slow.   *Author*

North Ings Farm Railway. A train on an open day, 22nd May, 1988. The Ruston locomotive, 'LAT' class, Works No. 421433, was delivered new to the Lincolnshire River Board in 1959 and was used by them in connection with engineering works in the maintenance of the banks of rivers and drains within the County. Disposed of in 1987 it was acquired by the North Ings Farm Railway where it is today.

One, Ruston 'LAT' class, Works No. 421433, came here in 1987. This had worked for the Lincolnshire River Board on drain and river maintenance all its working life and remains in working order.

The interest from a number of Open Days was such that when the extended line was completed in 1990 the site opened as a museum. Now there is a wide variety of steam and diesel locomotives as well as the track and equipment. The site is regularly open throughout the summer, details of which can be obtained from the Tourist Information Office in Sleaford.

Birchgrove Bulb Museum, Pinchbeck

The bulb industry of South Lincolnshire developed in the Fens around the Spalding area from 1870. This is that part of Lincolnshire which was administered by the former Holland County Council and the Dutch link survives to this day, both in the name of the local authority, South Holland District Council, and in the names of several of the main employers. Lincolnshire has traditionally enjoyed close links with Holland for over 300 years.

The traditional bulbs grown were those of the daffodil and the tulip. Daffodils, and a small number of tulips are still grown today but the days when large numbers of people would visit the area in the spring to see acres of bulbs in flower have long gone. Just after World War II up to 100,000 visitors would come each year to see 7,000 acres under production. The history of this activity is today told at the Birchgrove Garden Centre at Pinchbeck, just north of Spalding.

Bulbs were planted in October and flowered in April. The flowers were harvested for the cut flower trade. The tops then died down and the bulbs harvested in July. Through to the 1950s and 60s the railway played an important role, especially with the flower trade, ensuring the crop reached its markets all over Great Britain.

Pinchbeck Bulb Museum. A length of 'Jubilee' track at the Museum. This is typical of the prefabricated track sections produced for the War Department and subsequently used on narrow gauge railways countrywide. A five metre length of two ft gauge 9 lb. per yard rail, secured to six steel sleepers with clutchbolts. These panels could be manhandled easily. They were used both to form permanent tracks and also to make temporary sidings into or across fields. *Author*

As with potatoes the producers had to be able to get onto their land in the autumn and spring when it could be wet. Furthermore, it was important not to use heavy equipment as the soil should not be compacted. Some bulb producers used light railways, with wagons pushed by hand, as the link between the fields and the sheds and glasshouses where cleaning, sorting and packing took place.

The narrow gauge equipment they used was the same as the potato growers used. Examples can be seen at the Museum. Here, several pre-fabricated lengths of 2 ft gauge rail, in 18 ft sections, have been laid. Turntables were used to move round corners and, again, there are examples. The Museum also has the frames of two wagons, both constructed by Ducroo & Brauns, a Dutch manufacturer of light railways, locomotives and equipment.

The equipment at the Museum was obtained from an apple orchard in the West of England. None survived locally.

Vine House Farm, Deeping St Nicholas

The owner of this farm, Mr P.N. Watts, has a private museum of old farming equipment, mainly hand tools, used in the area. As part of this he has restored the old loading dock at the terminus of the former light railway on this farm. A short length of track runs up on to it and there are two wagons (*see page 130*). As part of the restoration the track and wagons were brought from North Wales but they are very typical of what was seen in Lincolnshire.

Although docks survive elsewhere in the County this is the only one with rails. The reason why they tended to be great playgrounds for children can clearly be seen. With a good length of rail and a good push some distance could be travelled. It could almost have been the white-knuckle ride of its day.

The dock may be seen with the permission of the owner.

Uses for Old Rails

Vine House Farm, Deeping St Nicholas. To increase storage capacity within the roof space of a shed. *Author*

Victoria Farm, Deeping St Nicholas. In use to block unauthorized vehicles entering fields. *Author*

Rails used as fence posts at *Terry Booth Farm, Amber Hill* and as fence rails near to *Lighthouse Farm* at *Sutton Bridge*.   *Author*

Rails from the former *Fleet Light Railway* now used as part of a gateway on Holbeach Marsh.
Author

Caudwell's Farm, Grainthorpe. Old rails used here in 2002 to protect the edges of a ramp, to a farm building at 'Tintown'.   *Author*

At Carrington rails are in use to support a good display of runner beans and as clothes posts.

Above & Below left: Cupe Horn, Grainthorpe and at *Terry Booth Farm, Amber Hill.* Cut up into five feet lengths for use as fence posts.   *Author*

Below right: The last use of this length of rail was in a Carrington farmyard to support a water tap.   *Author*

Poplars Farm, Holland Fen. Here, rails had been cut in longer lengths than elsewhere, 12 feet, to support fox-proof fencing around pheasant-rearing pens.

Author

Former *Lighthouse Farm* rails used to support a farm sign at *Nene Lodge Farm, Sutton Bridge.*

Author

Poplars Farm, Holland Fen. Perhaps the most unusual use is to support a gravestone previously
damaged by grazing cattle.   *Author*

Appendix One

List of Lincolnshire Potato Railways

Key: S - Steam Engine, D - Diesel Engine, P - Petrol loco or Paraffin, H - Horse, T - Tractor

Location	*Gauge (where known)*	*Maximum Mileage*	*Date of Construction*	*Date of Closure*	*Method of Working*
1. Flatts Farm, Alkborough		¼	1930s	?	H
2. Sawcliffe Farm, Roxby		7/10	?	?	H
3. North Moor Farm, Belton	2 ft	3	*c.*1915	*c.*1953	H
4. Hall Farm and Common Farm, West Butterwick	2 ft	2½	before 1925	1939	H
5. Bishopthorpe Farm, Tetney	2 ft 6 in. (?)	2⅗	before 1932	1949	H
6. Low Farm, Marshchapel		1¼	1938	1943	H
7. Clyde House Farm, Marshchapel		1¼	*c.*1935	*c.*1946	H
8. Caudwell's Farms, Grainthorpe and North Somercotes		11½	*c.*1924	1950	H
9. New Marsh Farm, Havenhouse	2 ft	3	1927	*c.*1949	H D
10. Nocton Estates	1 ft 11½ in.	23	1920	1969	S D H
11. West Fen Farm, Carrington	2 ft	1		by 1945	H
12. Wragg Hall Farm, Carrington	2ft	1		after 1945	H
13. Terry Booth Farm, Harts Grounds		½	late 1920s	mid-1950s	H
14. Chestnut House Farm, Amber Hill			nothing known		
15. Poplars Farm, Holland Fen		⅗		after 1937	H
16. Rectory and Six Hundreds Farms, East Heckington		4	early 1920s	1945	H
17. Reesons Farm, Little Hale		¼	by 1931	1941	H
18. Marsh Farm, Gosberton		1 1/10	?	*c.*1939	H
19. Manor Farm, Frampton	2 ft	1⅘	*c.*1912	*c.*1941	H
20. Lammings Marsh Farm, Fosstyke	2 ft	⅘	*c.*1912	*c.*1941	H
21. Leadenhall Farm, Holbeach St Marks		3 3/10	*c.*1914	*c.*1946	H
22. Wraggmarsh House, Weston	2 ft	6	before 1909	1947	P H
23. Moulton Marsh, Moulton		3	before 1914	1955	H
24. Majors Farm, Whaplode		3	before 1914	*c.*1951	P H

Location	Gauge (where known)	Maximum Mileage	Date of Construction	Date of Closure	Method of Working
25. Whaplode Marsh Farm, Saracen's Head, Whaplode		1¼	before late 1920s	c.1946	H
26. Manor House, Saracen's Head, Whaplode		1	after 1931	c.1950	H
27. Lundy's Farm, Holbeach St Marks	2 ft	1 7/10	1913	c.1950	H
28. Reckerby Farm, Holbeach St Matthew		1	?	c.1939	H
29. Lawyers Farm, Holbeach St Matthew	2 ft	3	late 1920s	early 1940s	H
30. Wards Farm, Holbeach St Matthew		1	c.1920	c.1940	H
31. Christie House Farm, Holbeach St Matthew		5/10	c.1920	c.1942	H
32. The Grange, Holbeach St Marks		7/10	before 1920	c.1942	H
33. Desert Farm, Holbeach Marsh		2	before late 1920s	c.1950	H
34. Fleet Light Railway, Fleet	2 ft	12 7/10	1910	1955	P D H
35. Thompson's, Dawsmere	2 ft	7 7/10	c.1921	1940	D H
36. Red House Farm, Dawsmere	2 ft	2	early 1920s	c.1939	H
37. Red House Farm, Gedney Dyke		½	?	early 1940s	H
38. Brook House Farm, Gedney Dyke		½	?	?	H
39. Lighthouse Farm, Sutton Bridge	2 ft	1 7/10	1926	1946	H
40. South Fen Farm, Bourne		7/10	mid-1920s	?	H
41. Tongue End Farm, Deeping St Nicholas		2 2/5	1923/4	c.1946	P H
42. Sixscore Farm, Deeping St Nicholas		1 3/10	late 1920s	c.1939	H
43. Carter's Farm, Deeping St Nicholas		1/5	late 1920s	c.1950	H
44. Victoria Farm, Deeping St Nicholas		1 3/10	c.1925	c.1949	H T
45. Hedge Farm, Deeping St Nicholas		2	before 1918	1944	H
46. Bottom Farm, Crowland	2 ft	1¼	before 1928	c.1935	H
47. Dennis Estates, Deeping St Nicholas	2 ft	10 1/10	by 1916	1950	H P
48. East Reach Farm, Deeping St Nicholas		1 1/5	before 1914	c.1945	H
49. Vine House Farm, Deeping St Nicholas	c.2 ft 2 in.	1 7/10	not known	c.1940	H
50. Caulton Farm, Deeping St Nicholas		3 3/10	c.1921	c.1950	H

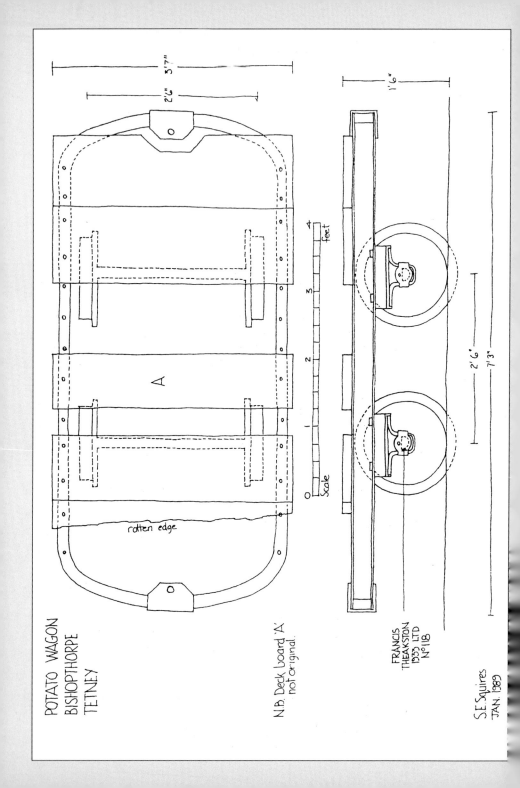

POTATO WAGON
BISHOPTHORPE
TETNEY

5'7"

2'6"

A

rotten edge

N.B. Deck board 'A'
not original.

1'6"

2'6"

7'3"

Scale

0 1 2 3 4 feet

FRANCIS
THEAKSTON
1955 LTD
Nº118

S.E. Squires
JAN. 1989

Appendix Two

The Bishopthorpe Wagon and Francis Theakston

This wagon is the only known wagon, other than those which were ex-War Department, found on any of the farms within this book. It was at Bishopthorpe Farm, Tetney on the line that once ran between Bishopthorpe and Low Farm. This line was in operation until 1949. The wagon lay discarded in the farmyard at Bishopthorpe in amongst a collection of other redundant farming equipment and implements. It was rediscovered in 1987.

As so often with these farm railways it is somewhat of an enigma. It was of 2 ft 6 in. gauge. What is not known is if this shows that the line here was of a wider gauge than the 2 ft found elsewhere or whether it was bought to be re-gauged for a 2 ft line but never carried out.

The wagon is very simple and robust in construction. In style it is similar to those used at Wraggmarsh House, Weston and Red House Farm, Dawsmere, for which photographic evidence survives. This is, perhaps, not surprising, as these were both farmed by George Caudwell, the brother of Robert Caudwell, of Bishopthorpe.

The wagon has a straight-sided but bow-ended steel frame. Beneath this are bolted two pairs of wheels. The frame is surmounted by a flat timber deck, again bolted to the frame. The axle boxes have a maker's name cast into them. This is 'Francis Theakston 1933 Ltd No 118'.

In 1988 a major exhibition was mounted at the Museum of Lincolnshire Life, in Lincoln. This was called 'Taates', the Lincolnshire dialect term for potatoes. The wagon was loaned by the Farm Manager to the Museum for the period of the exhibition and formed part of the display. With the closure of the exhibition the wagon was returned to the farm. Its subsequent future is unknown.

Francis Theakston was a light railway equipment manufacturer, from North Yorkshire. He was a member of the famous brewing family. As a young man he was trained for a career in engineering, partly at the Koppel works in Germany. Following the outbreak of World War I he worked for the War Office and was involved with the supply of equipment for the narrow gauge light railways laid in France to supply the front lines. He was, for a time, in charge of purchasing.

On the Western Front the need was for light, prefabricated lengths of track which could be laid and dismantled quickly. Theakston devised such a panel using 9 lb./yard rails. The rails were held together by tie bars rather than sleepers. The rails were punched at regular intervals to enable the tie bars to be fixed. Furthermore, the rails were fitted with the Theakston claw joint, a hook and catch system which enabled track sections to be clipped together.

After the war he started his own business in Crewe making light railway equipment. It is known that he supplied stock and equipment for the Ravenglass and Eskdale Railway and track for the Romney, Hythe & Dymchurch Railway. He advertised as manufacturing track, points and crossings, turntables, wagon tipplers, wagons and locomotives. Much went for export.

Perhaps not surprisingly, he was involved with the early developments in the use of internal combustion-engined locomotives on the narrow gauge. This had been given a big boost during his war service with the need to develop locomotives to work on the very light rail sections in use at the time. He had locomotives built in the 1920s by both Kerr, Stuart and Avonside, which he fitted with 'Theakston' plates with his Trade Name of UBIQUE.

Theakston's was eventually bought out by Robert Hudson & Co. of Leeds who continued to employ Francis at their London office. Hudson's were major manufacturers of narrow gauge railway equipment. An example of the frame and wheels of a flat wagon as supplied by them can be seen on the Lincolnshire Coast Light Railway.

Appendix Three

Christian & Dobbs

Christian & Dobbs were a firm of Ironmongers and Implement Agents who traded from premises in Long Sutton Market Place. Fred Christian and Leslie Dobbs, both from Pinchbeck West, started the business in 1923. Their aim was to serve the needs of farmers, farm workers and farms throughout the area.

Bartholomew Young Banks JP, of Sutton Bridge owned land in the Thorney area of Cambridgeshire, east of Peterborough. It was for him that they first built light railways. There were two light railways near here, both of 2 ft gauge and both running from Wryde station, in the Parish of Thorney, on the Midland and Great Northern Joint Railway. These may be the railways referred to. One of these ran from the station yard, where it had its own dock, across the road by an ungated level crossing to a shed alongside the road. The shed and rails in a concrete overbridge across the roadside dike still survive. The line then ran east and north for about one mile out into the fields. It was horse-worked with a number of flat wagons. The second, also horse-worked, ran south from the station for about half a mile.

Christian & Dobbs are also known to have supplied equipment for Lighthouse Farm at Sutton Bridge and for Clyde House Farm at Marshchapel, near Grimsby. It is likely, therefore, that they also supplied equipment for other farms. The track was not prefabricated or second-hand. A firm in Grantham supplied their rails with sleepers coming from the sawmill of W. Groom Ltd of Spalding. The firm would also lay the track if farm labour were not available.

The firm ceased trading in the early 1980s but their premises survive, still selling hardware. Their name, set in a coloured, leaded glass panel can still be seen above the door.

In 1923 the firm of Christian & Dobbs established their Ironmongery and Implement Agency in Long Sutton Market Place. The building is seen here in 2003.   *Author*

Now housing Parkway it still retains Art Nouveau glazing over the doors and windows incorporating the name of its original owners.   *Author*

Acknowledgments to First Edition

I had for many years known a little about the railways at Nocton and Fleet, and I had also been aware of two or three other very short lengths of track in the Holbeach area. Intrigued, I set out to find out all I could about them. It soon became apparent that I had only touched the tip of an iceberg. The total number surprised me, and I still would not claim to know them all. There may be others, and, if so, I would like to hear of them.

The work was a labour of love, made more enjoyable by the many people, mostly long-serving or retired farmers and their workers who welcomed me into their homes, gave me *carte blanche* to tramp their land, took me on conducted tours, and wrote to me at great length. In recognition of their help, I list them all below, together with the lines which they knew. I thank them all.

D.C. Atkinson: Victoria Farm; Michael Back: Fleet Light Railway; G.R. Bletcher: North Moor Farm; Harry Britton: Fleet Light Railway, Brook House Farm, Red House Farm, Gedney Dyke; A.W. (Sonny) Cobley: Tongue End Farm; P.K. Dennis: Dennis Estates railways; A. (Pop) Ellis: Hall Farm and Common Farm; Mr Ellis: Nocton Estates Manager; A.C. Fensom: Lawyers Farm; D. Hargrave: Caulton Farm; B.A. Johnson: Lundy's Farm; Ralph Kitson: North Moor Farm; Paul Lefevre: Nocton Estate; David Longmate: Nocton Estate; Roland Marshall: Agricultural history; Narrow Gauge Railway Society; Tom Neave: Thompson's, Dawsmere; David Piccaver: Thompson's, Dawsmere; G.H. Pickwell: Wraggmarsh House; Ron Redman: Nocton Estate; Bill Redshaw: Nocton Estate; David Sharpe: Lawyers Farm, Wards Farm, Red House Farm, Dawsmere; P.H. Shepherd: Fleet Light Railway; Eddie Sismey: Wraggmarsh House, Red House Farm, Dawsmere; G. Thompson: Reckerby Farm; H.C. Tinsley: Majors Farm, Moulton Marsh; Don Turner: Nocton Estate; Lewis Ward: Thompson's, Dawsmere; Len Waters: Leadenhall Farm, Majors Farm, Whaplode Marsh Farm; P.N. Watts: railways at Deeping St Nicholas; T. Wing: Lighthouse Farm; R.P. Worth: Grange Farm, Christie House Farm.

Acknowledgements to New Edition

As with the First Edition of this book, it would not have been possible to produce without the support, interest and enthusiasm of others. The First Edition sparked a lot of additional information and many people have contacted me over the last few years to volunteer what they knew. In addition, I have again been welcomed on farms all over the County by today's owners who have been as interested to hear what I knew and to seek out, in particular, many miles of rusting rails cut into fence posts and found not only around the fields but also tucked away inside farm buildings. To them all I am very grateful.

Again, as with the First Edition, if there are additional farm railways anyone knows about that are not included or if someone has additional memories, please contact me via the Oakwood Press.

Michael Back, Nocton, Littleworth; Dr Tom Bell, South Tynedale Railway Preservation Society; Dick Briggs; Terry Booth Farm; Chestnut House Farm, Poplars Farm; Hedley Butler, West Fen and Wragg Hall Farms, Carrington; R.G. Cash, LIFU Lorry and Town End Farm; Raymond Caudwell, Low Farm, Marshchapel; Martin Chapman, Grainthorpe; Gerry Cork, Amberley Chalk Pits Museum; Bob Darvill and the Industrial Railway Society, Locomotive History; C. Dawson, Havenhouse and Grainthorpe; Mike Gott, Lincolnshire Coast Light Railway; Donny Hall, Six Hundreds Farm; Late W. Hall, Bishopthorpe; George Hay, George Caudwell; Derek Hopper, Grainthorpe; Alan Hubbert, Bowsers, East Heckington; Late W. Hubbert, Bowsers, East Heckington; Tim Hudson, North Sea Camp and Lincolnshire River Board railways; J. and L. Hutton, Bowsers, East Heckington; Colin Judge; North Moor Farm; J.R. Laking, Pyes Farm; Mark Leggot, Terry Booth Farm, Chestnut House Farm, Carrington and Amber Hill; Alf Ludlam, Havenhouse; Walter McGrath, LIFU Lorry; E.P. Mossop, Marshchapel and Grainthorpe; Eileen Mumby, Nocton Estate Light Railway; John Nickols, Little Hale; Malcolm Phillips, North Ings Farm Railway; H. Reeson, Little Hale; Late Ron Redman, Equipment Manufacturers; Ian Rowson, Grainthorpe; George Slinger, Birchgrove Bulb Museum; Jim Smith, Lincolnshire Coast Light Railway; David Spain, Fleet Light Railway; Mike Stanyon, Swineshead; John Thornley, Havenhouse; Geoff Towell, Flatts Farm; Stephen Walker, Havenhouse; Tony Wall, North Sea Camp Railway; Nicholas Watts, South Fen Farm, Victoria Farm, Vine House Farm; Len Woodhead, Nocton Estate; John Wooley, Festiniog Railway.